Kuan Yin

Accessing the Power of the Divine Feminine

Daniela Schenker

SOUNDS TRUE
PO Box 8010   Boulder CO 80306-8010
Phone 800-333-9185   www.soundstrue.com

Sounds True is a trademark of Sounds True, Inc.,
PO Box 8010, Boulder, CO 80306.

Manufactured in China.

ISBN: 978-1-59179-621-3

Originally published as *Kuan Yin: Begleiterin auf den Spirituellen Weg*
© 2006 Hans-Nietsch-Verlag, Freiburg, Germany
Illustrations © 2006 Antonia Baginski
© 2007 all photography Daniela Schenker except p. 125 Brigitte Rathmanner
and p. 140 top right by Rolf Herkert

Grateful acknowledgement is made to the following for permission to reprint
excerpts from previously published material:
The Lotus Sutra, translated by Burton Watson, copyright 1993. Reprinted by
permission of Columbia University Press via the Copyright Clearance Center.

Library of Congress Cataloging-in-Publication Data
Schenker, Daniela. Kuan Yin : accessing the power of the Divine Feminine
Daniela Schenker. p. cm.
Includes bibliographical references.
ISBN 978-1-59179-621-3 (hardcover)
1. Avalokitesvara (Buddhist deity) I. Title. BQ4710.A8S34 2007
294.3'4211—dc22
2007022793

Acid-free/alkaline paper
First edition published 2006.

To the Great Tao and the Jewel in the Lotus

Contents

Foreword

We waited for three days . . . but still no baby. My friend was dilated, but the labor hadn't started. I know that all good things come to those who wait. However, it felt like we had been waiting . . . and waiting . . . and waiting.

I had flown from my home on the central coast of California across the country to Atlanta, Georgia, to be present for the delivery. Amber was 39 years old, and this was her first pregnancy. I had known her for a number of years—she felt like a soul sister to me—and I was honored to be asked to be the birth coach.

During those three days, we meditated and prayed about the coming birth. I also massaged acupressure points on her ankles to help initiate the contractions. I led her on guided visualizations and used hypnosis to facilitate the process. Her husband assured us that everything was packed and ready for the ride to the hospital. Yet the labor didn't start.

Amber's anticipation heightened; she was eager and prepared, and I had done everything I could think of to help start the process. I really wanted this to be the most magical, wondrous experience of her life. I just didn't know what else to do to get things going.

So I surrendered. Simply and utterly surrendered.

The act of "surrendering" has a mysterious magic of its own. In that moment of truly letting go, I felt forces beyond this realm nudge at my soul and the words "Kuan Yin" quietly emerged inside of me.

Kuan Yin! Of course! I thought. *She's the embodiment of the divine feminine forces of the universe. Childbirth has always been under her protection. That's it! It's time to call in the big guns!*

I hurried to my friend and said, "Come on. Let's call upon the divine goddess Kuan Yin to bring forth this baby!"

We decided to call her while we were immersed in water, so we lit candles, filled Amber's huge Jacuzzi, added essential oils and bath salts, and made mountains of bubbles. Then we both slid into the warm water until we were up to our breasts in fragrant, silken fluid. It was so primordial, yet seemed to carry us to a sacred and sublime realm.

The sweetness of the moment transported me back to the time when, as a young woman, I lived in a Zen Buddhist monastery for several years. Every day I sat on my *zabuton* with my legs crossed in the lotus position and meditated on the pure peace of the Buddha. Sometimes I sat on my meditation pillow for sixteen hours a day. My back and knees hurt, but then again, Buddha said that life was suffering. I thought that maybe—through my suffering—I could attain enlightenment. I hoped that if I could transcend the pain, I could reach Nirvana.

But one afternoon I had an experience that shifted my perception of suffering. I had taken time off to visit a local museum that had a large collection of statues of Buddha. In this collection, one particularly large statue caught my attention. When I looked at the plaque that described it, I found that it wasn't Buddha after all—it was a statue of Kuan Yin. As I looked into the compassionate eyes of the statue, everything seemed to slow down. Although she was made of carved wood and paint, her eyes seemed to be a hallowed entrance point into other dimensions. It was as if I could hear her say, "You don't need to suffer to grow, Denise. The path to the light can be filled with joy and bliss."

This was an awakening for me. Although I loved my time in the Zen monastery, I had been suffering from knee and back pain for two years, hoping to become enlightened. Suddenly, I realized that I no longer needed to adhere to the "no pain, no gain" belief about spiritual advancement. The goddess spoke to me through the statue of Kuan Yin, showing me a different way. Shortly afterward I moved out of the *zendo* to pursue growth in more sumptuous and joyous ways.

This is the feminine way. This is the path of Kuan Yin. She speaks to us from a depth of compassion. And she isn't just a metaphor, but a real, viable force that you can call upon for protection and healing. She also activates love of self, love of others, and love of god . . . for she is the feminine embodiment of love.

As we sat in the rosemary-scented water, we softly invoked the holy energy of this divine being. "Kuan Yin, goddess of compassion, overseer of healing and liberation, we call upon you to bring forth this child easily and joyously."

As I looked into Amber's eyes, it seemed that her face transformed for a minute—that the spirit of Kuan Yin, the divine feminine, descended upon her. The goddess was present. It was a splendid moment. Right after we got out of the tub, Amber's water broke. And, like the ocean surging, gently yet powerfully, the first true contraction flowed through her body and labor began . . . and later culminated in a beautiful baby girl named Leela.

It could have been a coincidence that the labor started right after invoking the spirit of Kuan Yin, or it could have been that the warm water brought on the first big surge . . . but the synchronicity was remarkable. I believe that the divine feminine spirit (embodied in Kuan Yin) is available to anyone at any time.

Whenever you need compassion, understanding, or grace in your life, call upon her.

In Daniela Schenker's special book you will be introduced to the true sprit of Kuan Yin, and you will learn how to activate this power for healing and protection. Her book carries the spirit and energy of this remarkable deity, and you can use the wonderful images in it for meditation and contemplation.

May Kuan Yin bring you immense joy, fluidity, and compassion. May you receive her protection and grace.

—DENISE LINN
Author of *Sacred Space* and *Soul Coaching*

Acknowledgments

First let me thank Kuan Yin herself. Many years ago, this wonderful bodhisattva gave me a great gift: a very personal vision that inspired me to write this book.

My deep gratitude goes to my longtime artist friend, Antonia Baginski. Thank you for your beautiful paintings, which convey Kuan Yin's spirit and form the visual core of this book.

You must all be worldly bodhisattvas—my U.S. publisher, Sounds True, and the editing team of Sheridan McCarthy and Stanton Nelson, as well as my German publishers and Jurgen Lipp of Wrage bookstore in Hamburg, Germany, who made decisive contacts. Your creative support and commitment have carried me and touched me very deeply.

Thank you, Denise Linn, for writing the foreword! I have always loved your strong spirit, which brings feminine wisdom into this world.

My deepest gratitude goes to calligraphy and Tai Chi master Julie Lim and feng shui master Dr. Jes Lim, who initiated me on the Taoist path that we have been jointly treading for more than twelve years.

I give heartfelt thanks to my husband, Frank, who accompanies me with ceaseless love—whether in person or in his heart—on my journeys around the world(s), and who has always encouraged me to follow my personal path. We have traveled together to visit Kuan Yin and participated in many beautiful ceremonies.

Thanks also to Payodhi, Mânia Antarielle, Hanako, and Stephen Quong for their support and inspiration.

Being a professional translator, my deep respect goes to Kumarajiva, the fourth-century scholar who translated the Lotus Sutra and many other sacred texts into Chinese. His masterly work contributed to the spread of the Kuan Yin texts in ancient times.

Finally, my deep gratitude goes to all the masters and teachers of the spiritual traditions, and to all other sentient beings for their auspicious support.

May this book inspire numerous pilgrimages in both inner and outer realms.

Namo Kuan Shih Yin Pusa!

∾ Introduction ∾

Kuan Yin —Traveling the Path of Compassion

I first met Kuan Yin, the goddess of healing and compassion, more than twelve years ago. I had been studying with Tai Chi and calligraphy master Julie Lim, and she gave me a golden pendant with Kuan Yin standing on a large lotus flower. On the back was an engraving from the Heart Sutra, a beloved Buddhist text that is associated with Kuan Yin. I was touched by the gift, and immediately intrigued. Kuan Yin's face had a mystical quality, reminding me a little of Mona Lisa's subtle smile. I felt an inner stirring. *Who is the goddess behind this lovely image,* I wondered, *and what might I learn from her?*

While I did not know it at the time, this small gift was just the first step on a wonderful journey that would take me to exotic sites around the world and deep places within myself. I became immersed in Kuan Yin's history and iconography. I traced her origins and evolution, and visited temples where I could connect with her more deeply. I read ancient texts that described and honored her. In time I realized that Kuan Yin had become my wise, loving, and compassionate companion on the spiritual path. By tuning in to her many manifestations I have grown spiritually and have had many joyful experiences.

Kuan Yin is a *bodhisattva*, a being who refrains from entering Nirvana in order to come to the aid of others. There are many bodhisattvas, but the way she became one is unique to her. Kuan Yin had led such a pure, compassionate, and virtuous life that the gate to the highest enlightenment—Nirvana—at last lay open before her. But as she stood at the verge of this final threshold in contemplation, she heard shouts and cries of suffering emanating from all sentient beings, spreading about her like a great wave. So profoundly was she moved by the pain of the world's beings that her heart began to shake, and she knew that she could not yet leave the world behind. And so it was that Kuan Yin took the vow of a bodhisattva: "I will not reach final liberation until all other beings have been liberated."

My heart was deeply touched when I read this tale, and the reason that I had experienced such an immediate, intuitive attraction to Kuan Yin became abundantly clear. One day, several years before I learned of Kuan Yin's existence, I had a very intense mystical experience. I was doing the dishes—a simple thing—when my awareness suddenly shifted, unfolding and expanding. In an instant, I was hearing the sounds of people everywhere. I could hear babies crying, people sighing, screaming, and laughing—I was enveloped in teeming waves of human sound, from the first breath at birth to the last sigh at passing. While it was a very strange experience, I wasn't afraid; instead, I felt moved by the seemingly infinite expressions of life I was experiencing, and sensed a special opening that I still feel today. Then, just as suddenly as the sounds had come to me, they began to weave together, blending and fusing into a single wave—a profound vibration that I knew to be the sound of the human world.

Imagine having had this experience long before I'd ever heard of Kuan Yin, and then learning the story of how she became a bodhisattva! My own personal "cosmic ear" experience led me to feel a deep bond with her, and propelled me to seek her everywhere.

So my connection with Kuan Yin stems from an intense internal experience. But many of the stories people tell me about their own connections to her are quite different. People call on Kuan Yin for many reasons—to keep them safe while traveling, or to bless them with children. I have heard tales of people who were cured of serious diseases after seeking her blessings. This compassionate goddess has many manifestations, as you will soon discover. Because of this, there are myriad ways in which we can invite her into our lives, and many dimensions to our experiences of her. Though her roots are in ancient India and China, today she can be found everywhere. There are figurines of her on altars in Israel, for example, and in Mexico and Brazil she sits side by side with "Maria," mother of Jesus.

I am fortunate to work as a translator—my profession takes me all over the world. When I was in Malaysia in 1999, I received a Kuan Yin mantra initiation from a Buddhist master there. He told me stories about her, describing how she has rescued sailors and helped parents to have children. Then he told me that people often keep statues of Kuan Yin in their homes, and asked me if I would like to buy one.

The small shop he recommended to me was bursting with goods—from rice cookers and incense to the "ghost money" that is used as a symbolic offering in that country during burial ceremonies. Amid this potpourri, several large Kuan Yin statues gazed serenely.

I saw a standing Kuan Yin figurine made of pink porcelain, holding a fragile lotus flower in her hand. Another stood on a pedestal of bubbling water, carrying in her hands the nectar vase that is her "trademark." Through my work with the feng shui master Dr. Jes Lim, I had developed a keen interest in Asian culture and an eye for Asian aesthetics, so I was more than open to the power of these works of art. Delighted with my find, I bought three statues, each elegantly packaged in a brocade-covered box. Only then did I ask myself how in the world I would get them home.

South Sea Kuan Yin: Famous landmark of the Chinese island of Putuo Shan.

Kuan Yin helped me with the answer. When the moment came to transport my beautiful statues, I fervently asked her for help. With full concentration, I recited her mantra. Although my bag was very large, I managed to get through the security check. When I boarded the plane I had to pass the bag with its fragile contents to the flight attendant, and was a bit worried about what would happen next. A little later another flight attendant came to see me and smiled. The cabin crew had found a space; Kuan Yin was traveling first class! The largest of these lovely figurines is almost twenty inches tall and is now the centerpiece of the altar in my home.

I tuned in to Kuan Yin again and again in other parts of the world; she never failed to give me hints about where she could be found. While riding in a taxi in Sydney in 2001, I saw a highway sign bearing the strange name, "Wollongong." Following my intuition, I asked about this unusual name. The driver told me that this coastal town was home to a well-known Buddhist temple. I immediately changed my plans, asked the driver to turn around, and was soon on my way to the largest Chinese Buddhist temple in the Southern Hemisphere—filled, of course, with beautiful granite carvings of Kuan Yin.

The coincidences did not stop there. On a visit to Chinatown in Los Angeles the following year, my husband and I found a colorful disk-shaped picture of Kuan Yin embedded with a recording of her mantra. While I was looking at it, a store security guard standing nearby asked me whether I knew about the large Kuan Yin temple in the mountains outside the city.

The enormous Hsi Lai Temple nestles into a mountain in accord with feng shui principles: the land it sits upon is shaped like a bodhi tree leaf (it was under a bodhi tree that the Buddha attained enlightenment) and the mountain rises up behind it, protecting its back. The temple grounds provide a wonderful view of the city, which becomes a glittering sea of lights in the evening. I return there whenever I am in Los Angeles to connect with the magnificent power of Kuan Yin. The temple holds frequent rituals and sutra readings, as well as a three-hour ceremony dedicated to Kuan Yin once a month. I have been to this "Great Dharani of Compassion" ritual several times, and each time it is as beautiful and touching as the first. A *dharani* is a long mantra, most powerful when recited aloud. The polyphonic chanting of more than three hundred nuns and other worshippers is extraordinary, especially when combined with bells and the huge singing bowl near the altar. The sound, along with the repeated prostrations of so many people, creates a huge energy field in which Kuan Yin is especially tangible. It is very moving to experience the vibrant power of the large procession as it winds around rows of prayer cushions while everyone recites the ancient dharani. When it is over, each person receives a small bottle of Kuan Yin water, charged with the healing vibrations of the invocations.

I occasionally run into the security guard who first told me about the temple, and I enjoy hearing his stories. He once told me about an experience he had with Kuan Yin on a plane. There was a terrible thunderstorm, and he clearly saw her standing on one of the plane's wings. As he watched, her body suddenly disappeared, but he could still make out her footprint on the wing, adorned by the Buddhist dharma wheel. He is sure that she was there to protect the travelers and ensure that the plane would land intact.

On Kuan Yin's birthday in April 2002, I joined the many people who had gathered in front of the gates of Hsi Lai Temple for a walking meditation that turned out to be a great gift. I assumed that we would recite mantras while walking up the hill to the main shrine, but there was a much more demanding practice in store. Instead of merely walking, we were to do a certain kind of prostration, a practice described in one of the Kuan Yin legends. While reciting the mantra, each person was to take two steps, bow down, and touch the floor with the hands or the forehead. This process was to be repeated for the entire walk to the shrine. Accompanied by drums and bells, we took almost two hours to reach the main shrine on the mountain. I found this practice to be a special blessing. (My husband has good memories of the experience, too, despite being tormented by sore muscles for several days afterward.) It was at this point that I finally decided to take the famous pilgrimage to Mount Kailash in Tibet, a holy place in Buddhism and somewhere I had long wanted to visit. Kuan Yin's walking meditation was a signal to me that I had the stamina to tackle the ritual walk around the sacred mountain.

I continued to travel to meet Kuan Yin, including trips to San Francisco and New York, Thailand, Singapore, and two visits to the Chinese island of Putuo Shan, a magical place known to be Kuan Yin's main residence.

In addition to taking trips to visit Kuan Yin, I began to immerse myself in the study of her origins. I was surprised to discover that she originated in India in a very different form than she takes today. In fact, the tremendous variety of her forms is probably beyond anyone's grasp, as the ancient texts say that she has the ability to appear as almost anything—as a monk, a rich woman, or even a snake goddess. She will assume whatever form is required to teach compassion and respectful coexistence, and to heal. Over the course of centuries, Kuan Yin moved along the Silk Road from India to China and Southeast Asia. As I began to study her iconography, I was overwhelmed by the diversity of her forms—

Left: Richly colored porcelain figurines at a Chinese department store— typical of Chinatowns anywhere in the world.

nearly fifty in all plus various modern interpretations. While most retain the Chinese flavor of her more recent history, some point to her Indian roots, including one manifestation known as Kuan Yin with the Blue Neck. In this form, her coloring is reminiscent of the Hindu god Shiva who emptied a vial filled with poison that had the power to extinguish all life on earth.

As I spent more time with Kuan Yin and learned more about her, I developed an inner vision: I saw myself making her abundant variety of forms accessible to Western readers, offering images and contemplations to serve as gateways to a direct experience of her limitless compassion.

I told my longtime friend Antonia Baginski about my vision. She grasped the concept immediately, joined me in long discussions, and spent her own time tuning in to Kuan Yin. With sensitivity and grace, she applied her study of Asian art and her interpretation of its complexities to the project, creating thirty-three paintings of Kuan Yin in beautiful, radiant colors.

We both wanted to develop the feminist energy of Kuan Yin and convey it to Western readers. Although the ancient texts often refer to male representations of the deity, we portrayed her as she is most commonly known today, showing her exclusively in female form. She is not only the embodiment of the Buddhist ideal of compassion, the mighty healer who carries the nectar of healing and compassion in her vase; she is also an example of the powerful energy of the women who have preserved feminine ideals over the centuries despite the constraints of the male-dominated societies in which they have lived. The richly colored paintings and specially developed contemplations in this book will help you learn more about the wide range of images and their origins. And whether you are a woman or a man, they will help you to recognize and awaken your own varied energies and potential.

So it is that I welcome you, dear readers, to *Kuan Yin: Accessing the Power of the Divine Feminine*. I look forward to helping you connect with this goddess of compassion, whose spirit radiates throughout the world. My intention is for this book to serve as your pathway to her—a pathway strewn with images, legends, meditations, and mantras to aid you on your journey. I will begin by introducing you to Kuan Yin as she is found in both Eastern and Western traditions. Thirty-three images for contemplation follow, with accompanying text to help deepen your experience. A chapter on connecting with Kuan Yin offers practices designed to help you tune in to her. I will pass along some of the most famous stories and legends about Kuan Yin that I have heard. And finally, we'll take a quick visit to Putuo Shan, her island residence.

May the presence and power of Kuan Yin transform you as she continues to transform me.

DANIELA SCHENKER
Full moon in July (Guru-Poornima) 2007

Ethereal hands: Detail of a Japanese Kuan Yin stele.

Kuan Yin in Eastern and Western Traditions

 Kuan Yin is a fascinating and complex figure, an archetype of boundless compassion with roots in India. Over the course of a thousand years, her influence spread to other Asian countries, at first in male and then female form. Today, she reaches people in most parts of the world. But why does she resonate so strongly with people everywhere?

Kuan Yin in Eastern Spirituality
— The Bodhisattva Ideal —

In Buddhist tradition, bodhisattvas are enlightened beings who have attained the wisdom of buddhas but have postponed their final liberation; instead, they provide compassionate support to sentient beings in this world until all of them can achieve their own liberation. Ancient scriptures describe the moment when Kuan Yin became a bodhisattva: as she stood at the threshold to Nirvana, the cries of pain and suffering emanating from the world touched her compassionate heart, and she could not bring herself to leave it.

The bodhisattva ideal originates in the Mahayana tradition, one of the two main streams of Buddhism. Mahayana Buddhism spread primarily throughout Northeast Asia, China, and Tibet. It has influenced larger Buddhist movements such as Tibetan Buddhism, Zen Buddhism in Japan, and Pure Land Buddhism in China, where Kuan Yin plays an important role.

Altar of Tin Hao: The Chinese Queen of Heaven has strongly influenced Kuan Yin's evolution into a female figure.

People on the Mahayana path are not only expected to concentrate on reaching buddhahood, but also on developing compassion and helping other beings on the path. It is this, not one's own striving for enlightenment, that is the focus of spiritual development.

Buddhas and Bodhisattvas in Mahayana Buddhism

THE HISTORICAL BUDDHA	FIVE DHYANI BUDDHAS	BODHISATTVAS
Gautama	(Meditation Buddhas) Amitaba is one of these. He rules over the Pure Land where people who have left the cycle of rebirths are born. From the Pure Land they can attain buddhahood	Avalokiteshvara Kuan Yin Many others

The ancient scriptures describe two types of bodhisattvas—the worldly and the transcendent—as well as ten bodhisattva stages. The earthly bodhisattvas are embodied as humans, and they support their fellow beings on earth. We may think of Mother Teresa or the Dalai Lama as examples. Even Mozart can be seen as one, as a bodhisattva's activity does not have to be restricted to a religious context.

After the sixth stage, bodhisattvas reach the transcendent level; once they attain the highest stage, they are called *mahasattva*. They have achieved enlightenment but are still active in this world, endowed with special powers and the ability to act beyond natural laws. They may be called upon for help at any time.

Kuan Yin is a female mahasattva.

Avalokiteshvara: The Origin of Kuan Yin

Kuan Yin's origins can be found in India, in the male form of Avalokiteshvara, one of the great bodhisattvas described in sacred sutra texts. There are several legends about his birth and life. The Lotus Sutra says that he had 357 incarnations before he became a bodhisattva. According to other sutra texts, he was born from a ray of light that emanated from the right eye of Buddha Amitabha while he was in a state of ecstasy. When Avalokiteshvara was born, he held a lotus in his hand and spoke the mantra "Om Mani Padme Hum"—translated as "Om, the jewel in the lotus." (This mantra and the lotus symbol were later connected to the female Kuan Yin as well.) Avalokiteshvara will play an important role in the distant future, as it is predicted that one day, when Buddha Amitabha has finally reached Nirvana, Avalokiteshvara will take over his position to become Maitreya, the Buddha of the coming age.

— The Thousand-Armed Avalokiteshvara —

A legend describes Avalokiteshvara vowing not to rest until he has freed all sentient beings from the cycle of rebirth (in Sanskrit,

Above: Powerful helper: Magnificent thousand-armed Avalokiteshvara. Bangkok.

Below: Nine-Headed Kuan Yin: Enthroned under a dome of countless golden hands. Shanghai.

samsara. He travels to the hell realms, liberates those he finds there, and leads them to the Pure Land of his spiritual father, Amitabha. But despite his committed work, he finds that there are still innumerable unhappy beings still to be liberated. Each time he empties the hells, it takes only moments for them to fill again with newly reborn beings. So desperate is he, and so filled with grief and pain in the face of this overwhelming task, that his head bursts into eleven parts. But Amitabha swiftly comes to the aid of his son and transforms each fragment into an entire head. Now the bodhisattva has twenty-two eyes with which to identify suffering and eleven brains to find the best remedy to liberate all beings! When Avalokiteshvara returns to his task, however, he finds that his arms have fallen into pieces as well. Amitabha again works quickly to support his struggling son, and provides him with a thousand arms with which to carry on the massive task he has chosen.

Later representations of the female Kuan Yin appear with multiple arms and heads as well.

The Bodhisattva Vow

All beings, without number, I vow to liberate
Endless blind passions I vow to uproot
Dharma gates beyond measure I vow to penetrate
The way of the Buddha I vow to attain

— Avalokiteshvara and Kuan Yin in the Sutras —

Avalokiteshvara and Kuan Yin are mentioned in a multitude of sutras and are often their central focus. The male form, Avalokiteshvara, is usually preferred in the Indian texts. In later Chinese translations, the Kuan Yin form is found more frequently.

The Heart Sutra is considered to be one of the most important Buddhist texts. In it, Avalokiteshvara appears and imparts the transcendent spiritual experience of being. His central message is *emptiness is form and form is emptiness*. Ultimately, there are no sensory perceptions, no reaching or nonreaching, no aging, and no death. This insight creates fearlessness and eliminates illusions and attachments. Today, the core message of the Heart Sutra is frequently found on jewelry pendants like the one my teacher gave to me. On the back of the pendant, Kuan Yin is pictured carrying her nectar vase.

The twenty-fifth chapter of the Lotus Sutra extensively describes Avalokiteshvara in a multitude of manifestations. From this, thirty-three classical Chinese-Japanese forms have evolved, and many of these inspire the thirty-three contemplation images you will find in Chapter 2. The text is still used today as the basis of ceremonies and invocations of Kuan Yin; these sutras hold great spiritual power.

The Avatamsaka Sutra describes a pilgrim who meets more than fifty enlightened beings on his path. He visits the island of Putuo Shan in China, which is considered to be Kuan Yin's earthly home.

In the Shurangama Sutra, Avalokiteshvara describes how to transcend the sensory perception of hearing, and thus reach enlightenment. This sutra has special significance, and you will find a discussion of it on page 111.

— Kuan Yin Is Transformed in China —

There are probably many reasons that the male Avalokiteshvara was transformed into a female figure in China. He received his new name when master translator Kumarajiva rendered the Lotus Sutra into Chinese. He translated Avalokiteshvara as "Kuan-shih-yin": the one who perceives the sounds of the world.

Boundless compassion and helpfulness, which are seen as the main attributes of Avalokiteshvara, were considered feminine virtues. And it was mainly female laypeople who were interested in the exotic new bodhisattva from India and began to worship him. The sutra texts say that he can be invoked easily and, unlike Chinese gods, will immediately provide the protection and help described in Buddhist scriptures and legends.

Certainly, spiritually oriented women felt the need to connect with a being of the same gender, one they could turn to when they wished for sons or needed protection from diseases and dangers. Much like the Chinese Great Mother, Kuan Yin was especially worshipped by women, whose role was severely curtailed in male-dominated Confucianism. More and more, the figurines and images of Kuan Yin assumed female features. Some transitional images even show Kuan Yin in feminine robes, but sporting a fine moustache! Popular legends and miracle tales that at first described Kuan Yin as a monk would now tell of a white-robed woman. By the ninth century AD, practically all images of Kuan Yin were female. This probably indicates that the Chinese collective consciousness had strongly absorbed the bodhisattva in female form.

Kuan Yin's Evolution in Chinese Tradition

Taoism evolves
(Ancient cultures of China, e.g., Hemudu, Longshan, etc.)
About 7000 BC

The goddess and god of creation are half-human, half-animal. Rituals are used to obtain the mercy of the forces of nature. Natural phenomena are interpreted as omens. Taoist gods and mother goddesses such as the Empress of Heaven evolve further.

Zhou Dynasty
About 700 BC

First Buddhist influences come from India to China. The Chinese princess Miao Shan, who is later considered to be an embodiment of Kuan Yin, lives during this time.

Han Dynasty
206 BC–AD 207

The Lotus Sutra is brought from India to China. It is considered one of the most important texts of Mahayana Buddhism, featuring Bodhisattva Avalokiteshvara in an important role.

Jin Dynasty AD 265-420	The Heart Sutra is translated into Chinese. Worship of the male Avalokiteshvara ("Kuan-shih-yin" in Chinese) begins.
Sui Dynasty AD 581–618	Avalokiteshvara is worshiped more widely, depicted as a graceful male or androgynous being. The first legends and miracle stories appear.
Tang Dynasty AD 618-907	Buddhism is introduced to Japan and Korea in the sixth century. First Christian missionaries arrive in China by 635. In 705 the Shurangama Sutra is translated into Chinese; it describes Avalokitesvara attaining enlightenment through the sense of hearing. The first female images of Kuan Yin appear; she is also called Mother of the Ten Thousand Buddhas. Princess Miao Shan is regarded as an incarnation of Kuan Yin. Many stories and legends of Kuan Yin in her female form appear. The figure of White-Robed Kuan Yin spreads during the eighth century.
Song Dynasty AD 960–1279	Female images of Kuan Yin are now found in most Buddhist, Taoist, and Confucian temples. By the tenth century, the male image of Avalokiteshvara has practically disappeared.
Ming Dynasty AD 1368–1644	The legend of Princess Miao Shan spreads further. Monks settle on the Chinese island of Putuo Shan. Missionaries start to spread Christanity in Japan, where Kuan Yin is worshipped as the transitional god/goddess Kannon. Hybrid figurines of Mary-Kannon evolve.
Quing Dynasty AD 1644–1911	Jesuits bring images of Mary to China, inspiring changes in images of Kuan Yin.

Examples of different image styles.

17

There was a rapid rise in female figurines of Kuan Yin in response to the legend of the Chinese princess Miao Shan, who is known to have lived during the seventh century BC. She was so pious and so compassionate toward people that she proved an exemplary embodiment of Kuan Yin, and due to her tremendous popularity, countless variations of her story have evolved. The following tale is an example.

— The Legend of Princess Miao Shan —

There once was a king who had three daughters. The youngest was named Miao Shan, meaning "wonderful virtue." At the moment of her birth, the earth shook, the sky rained down flowers, and a delicate scent filled the air around her. Many people said that these signs indicated a most sacred incarnation.

But the king and the queen cared little about this—they were both very greedy. The only thing they wanted was to acquire as much material wealth as possible, and they found it difficult to understand this little girl, who was pure of heart and focused exclusively on virtuous deeds.

When Miao Shan grew up, her father expected her to marry. But she resisted his decision and said she would only be married if it would help her to free humanity from suffering. If this was not to be, her aim was to continue her spiritual practice and use it to help all sentient beings, both humans and animals.

When the king learned that his daughter refused to marry, he was furious, and he tried to punish her by making her perform menial tasks. Her sisters and her mother tried to persuade her to bow to her father's wishes, but in vain. Finally, the king threw up his hands and sent Miao Shan to live in a monastery.

He ordered the nuns there to make his daughter perform only the most difficult and backbreaking tasks and to treat her so poorly that she would change her mind and submit to his will. The girl was forced to carry wood and water and build a garden in barren soil. Thanks to the devoted efforts of the young nun, the land turned into a paradise. Miao Shan lovingly tended all the plants so well that the garden became lush and even retained its splendor during winter.

Apparently from nowhere, a spring emerged—very close to the kitchen. And the animals began to assist Miao Shan in carrying out her labors.

When the king heard about these miracles, he flew into a rage; he wanted to kill Miao Shan. He had told the nuns to force her to her knees, and in that they had failed in their task, they, too, deserved to die. The king gave orders to burn down the monastery, including all its occupants. But when Miao Shan saw that the building was on fire, she pierced her tongue with a hairpin—soon blood began to shoot from it. This summoned heavy storm clouds, and it started to rain. The fire was extinguished, and the nuns were saved.

The king refused to give up, and to get rid of his daughter once and for all he decided to have Miao Shan executed. But no weapon could kill her: she was protected by the celestial Jade Emperor himself, the ruler of heaven. Sword after sword, arrow after arrow broke before they could touch her body. Then, suddenly, the air became very still, and a huge white tiger appeared. He grasped Miao Shan and then bounded away with a single giant leap.

It was in this way that Miao Shan reached the intermediate worlds and met Yama, the ruler of the hell realms. He led her to their chambers, which were filled with the suffering cries of all beings. Miao Shan sent her deepest compassion to the crying ones. One by one they were liberated by her empathy, and the hells filled with light, music, and wonderful scents. Yama had to send Miao Shan away, as powers like hers had no place in the hells. As she was leaving, he gave her a peach of longevity as a gift.

Miao Shan now flew through the air and reached the island of Putuo Shan, where she remained in deep meditation for many years. During this period she lived only on the dew of grasses and the scent of flowers.

Then one day when she was deep in meditation, she saw the image of her father in the last stages of severe illness. The doctors were helpless: her father could neither sleep nor eat—he would soon die.

Suddenly, a monk appeared at the king's court and promised to heal him. To achieve this, however, he would have to prepare a special medicine from the eyes and arms of a human who had experienced neither anger nor hatred. This type of being, the monk said, a bodhisattva who would joyously fulfill his request, lived on the island of Putuo Shan. The king sent a messenger, who soon found the bodhisattva. Miao Shan was happy to give her arms and eyes; they were prepared into medicine that instantly brought about the king's recovery.

The king tried to thank the monk, but the monk told him that only the being who had selflessly given of its own body deserved the king's gratitude. Then he disappeared as suddenly as he had come. The king decided to travel with his wife to Putuo Shan to bring a wonderful gift to the mysterious, life-saving donor.

When the king and queen found the cave where the bodhisattva dwelled, they discovered that this miraculous being was their daughter, Miao Shan. At the moment of recognition the air became filled with a delicate scent, and flowers rained down from the ceiling. The cave was bathed in brilliant light as Miao Shan transformed into her sacred manifestation with a thousand eyes and arms and then floated away. She had become the embodiment of the purest unconditional compassion.

Humbled and in gratitude, her parents began their own spiritual practice and meditation. They built a shrine in the place where they had reunited with their daughter. Today it is known as Fragrant Mountain.

Kuan Yin in Western Spirituality

Though her roots are in Asia, Kuan Yin's radiant compassion has reverberated throughout the West, and I have been surprised to find connections to her in Western metaphysical philosophy. Here are two examples that I have found in my exploration.

— Kuan Yin in the Theosophical Teachings —

Theosophy (from the Greek, meaning "divine wisdom") is the universal attempt of cultures to understand the divine and delve into the evolutionary plan. Since antiquity, theosophical teachings have dealt with mysticism, astrology, esoterics, occult studies, and other attempts to attain a higher truth. Ancient records of the evolved sages and masters of humankind provide an important orientation to these teachings.

Theosophy holds that human beings are composed of various vehicles and energies that are subject to the laws of karma and reincarnation. Everything that exists in the universe—which is without beginning and end—is related to cosmic consciousness and is animated and inspired by it. Thus, all beings are connected in an indivisible universal brotherhood.

Nan Tien Temple in Woolongong, Australia.

The founder of the Theosophical Society, Helena Blavatsky (1831–1891), stands out among Theosophists because of her pivotal book *The Secret Doctrine*, a synthesis of science, religion, and philosophy. In the book Blavatsky repeatedly mentions Kuan Yin (also known as Kwan Yin), whom she considers the female logos and the divine voice of the soul. Blavatsky describes Kuan Yin's role as Maitreya Buddha of the coming age, as well as her versatility beyond any gender. Further, Kuan Yin appears in the book as the "inspiring spirit or genius of the water."

— Kuan Yin as Ascended Master —

Alice Bailey (1880–1949) is considered one of the outstanding personalities of the esoteric movement. She said that she was in psychic contact with the Tibetan master Djwhal Khul, who transmitted many books to her over a period of several years. Bailey's teachings are strongly inspired by the books of Helena Blavatsky and other theosophical practitioners. According to Bailey, there is a group of ascended masters on this earth who play a decisive role in the spiritual development of humankind. Ascended masters are similar

Staircase leading to the pagoda and granite statue at the Nan Tien Temple in Wollongong, Australia.

Kuan Yin in the West: Today there are Buddhist temples in the United States, England, the Netherlands, Australia, and many other countries. Left and Center: Nan Tien Temple, Wollongong, Australia. Right: Hsi Lai Temple, Los Angeles.

to bodhisattvas; they are human souls who no longer need to reincarnate on earth, as they have reached the level of mastery, but they have decided to stay in touch with humans. Because of their experiences over many lifetimes, they are very loving and patient teachers who support humanity on its path toward the light and back to the source. We can get in touch with them simply by sincerely asking them for help—it is not necessary to pray to them or submit to them in any way.

Apart from Kuan Yin, some of the better-known ascended masters are Jesus, Mary, St. Germain, and Gautama Buddha. Among the masters, Kuan Yin is the custodian of the Temple of Mercy. This place of light exists on a subtle level that is not visible to the human eye. It is said to be located over Beijing in China, according to some sources, and above the island of Putuo Shan according to others.

Kuan Yin is also a member of what Bailey refers to as the "Karmic Council." This is a group of light beings at the highest level who are able to use the Akashic Record to retrieve all types of information from the human world. We can invoke ascended master Kuan Yin and ask her to release personal karma, negative vibrations, and programming, and to lift our bodies to a higher vibrational level.

Amitabha
Spiritual father of Avalokiteshvara and Kuan Yin

Avalokiteshvara
Male bodhisattva of compassion in India and Tibet

Transformation into female form

Kuan Yin
Female bodhisattva of compassion in China

Chinese Niang-Niang goddesses and the Heavenly Empress Tin Hau
Protectors from the dangers of the oceans and diseases

Kuan Yin and Her "Sisters"

In both East and West there are female idols very similar to Kuan Yin. The most widely known of these are Tara and Mary.

—Tara—

Tara was originally the Indian star goddess (*tara* is Sanskrit for "star"). Depicted with bare breasts and a narrow waist, she sits on a lotus flower holding three more lotus flowers (symbolizing the three different levels of enlightenment). In various manifestations, Tara has belonged to the pantheon of Indian Mahayana Buddhism since the third century AD. In the eighth century she was introduced into Tibet. Her Japanese name is Tarani Bosatsu, whose manifestation is light green; she holds a lotus and a pomegranate (representing prosperity). This figure is a fusion of Green Tara and White Tara from the Tibetan tradition.

There are many different legends about the origin of Tara. One of them describes Avalokiteshvara being so overwhelmed by his task as a bodhisattva that two tears ran from his eyes, becoming a white tara and a green tara who would support him as his helpers.

Like Kuan Yin, Tara embodies the ideal of a female being attaining enlightenment. According to the Tara-Tantra texts, Tara incarnated as the Indian princess Jnânacandrâ (wisdom moon) who worked tirelessly for the benefit of sentient beings and gave donations to ordained monks and nuns. When she had reached a high level of realization, one of the monks mocked her, saying that from then on she should consciously reincarnate in a male body, since the body of a female posed more obstacles to enlightenment. The princess answered that, in absolute truth, there was no such thing as male and female, and vowed that she would incarnate exclusively as a woman in order to become enlightened in a female body. After she showed that it was possible to reach enlightenment as a female, Tara became known in Tibet as the "Savioress" or "Liberator," and has provided inspiration for generations of spiritual practitioners of both genders ever since.

Left: The White Tara: Embodiment of wisdom and longevity.
Right: Statue of Mary in a cave at the Lake Shrine, Los Angeles.

— Mary —

Mary and Kuan Yin both embody the feminine ideal of compassion. At first sight, they resemble each other; both wear loosely fitting flowing robes that cover and hide their bodies. They also share flower symbols: while the rose is associated with Mary, the lotus is attributed to Kuan Yin`s purity and enlightenment. On the other hand, Mary and Kuan Yin seem to represent the complementing polarities of yin and yang. While Mary is very gentle and unobtrusive, quietly following the Christ, Kuan Yin in her most active form has a thousand arms and myriad remedies that she uses to immediately come to the aid of suffering beings. Both divine mother figures enjoy worldwide worship by large numbers of people.

At the same time that Kuan Yin was emerging as a female figure in China, the image of Mary began to be spread there by Christian missionaries. Both gained popularity and acceptance during the seventh century, sharing iconographic similarities. The people sensed the closeness between the two spiritual "sisters," sometimes even confusing images of Mary brought by foreign visitors as gifts with those of Kuan Yin. Chinese artists were inspired by statues and images of

Mary, and later the Renaissance Madonna and Child, and integrated iconographic features such as the veil into the works of art depicting Kuan Yin.

Kuan Yin became protector of Japanese Christians, who faced centuries of official persecution. They made use of her similarity to Mary, worshipping her image while pretending to be Buddhists and hiding their pictures of Christian saints inside Buddhist statues. There was even a type of hybrid statue that evolved, resembling the Kuan Yin with Children form of the bodhisattva and carrying a concealed Christian cross.

In modern times, in East and West, quite a few altars hold both Mary and Kuan Yin figurines, evidence of their sisterly task in the world and the dialogue between the two religions.

Thirty-three Images
for Contemplation

 Images of Kuan Yin communicate directly with our spiritual selves, on both conscious and subconscious levels. They bring her love and compassion into our lives while reminding us that we, too, have the power to offer love and compassion to others.

The many representations of Kuan Yin can be traced back to two different sources: the sutras of Mahayana Buddhism and Chinese and Indian folklore. Those that are inspired by Buddhism may show her in supernatural form, with multiple heads and many arms, whereas folklore images such as Kuan Yin with Children or Dragonfish Kuan Yin are more representative of the natural world. In both cases, though, we find such symbols as the willow twig and nectar vase, both of which represent healing and compassion, and the lotus flower, a symbol of purity and enlightenment.

Chinese depictions of Kuan Yin have been inspired by Chapter 25 of the Lotus Sutra, a well-known Buddhist text. It describes Avalokiteshvara's multiple forms, which were very popular during the Sui (581–618 AD) and Tang (618–907 AD) dynasties in China. Woodblock prints and paintings of them were gathered into collections of thirty-three pictures each. (Thirty-three is a symbolic number in Chinese tradition, meaning "numerous.")

The thirty-three images you will find here were chosen from among Kuan Yin's many manifestations. They are based on Asian models, but they also bear a touch of Western art. Despite the fact that the sutra texts usually describe Kuan Yin as male, she has been worshipped in her female form for centuries, and representing her as female in this book was a conscious choice; it serves to

connect Kuan Yin's ancient message with our current Aquarian New Age, the age of women.

Each of the two-page spreads that follow is designed to give you several ways to access Kuan Yin for meditation and contemplation. You may choose to connect intuitively with the image itself—each carries its own subtle messages and vibrations. Take in the colors and the tone of the piece, and notice the many symbols you see: what Kuan Yin is wearing, what she holds in her hands, and the elements that surround her. (The meanings of these symbols are described in Appendix B, beginning on page 154).

Because the special qualities of Kuan Yin's manifestations are universal, the accompanying text encompasses both Asian and Western viewpoints. Each page of text begins with a key word: a succinct description of the essence of the form that can help you get straight to the heart of its meaning. Then the unique qualities and special powers of the particular form are described. You will find thumbnail sketches of stories and legends that are associated with several of the forms. (Longer versions of some of these can be found in Chapter 4, Tales and Legends of Kuan Yin, beginning on page 127.) Excerpts from the Lotus Sutra accompany most of the images. I have chosen to preserve the authenticity of the translations, retaining references to the bodhisattva as "he" and "him," as these passages really transcend gender. Each page ends with a contemplation that offers an example of how you can honor Kuan Yin and bring her special insights and powers into your life.

You may choose an image spontaneously, by opening this section of the book at random, or you may consciously select an image that you feel attracted to at the moment. Once you have selected your Kuan Yin, you may want to leave the book open to those pages, placing it in a spot where you can catch glimpses of her throughout the day. In this way, her energy will flow continuously into your life.

May Kuan Yin support you on your path!

1

Dragonhead Kuan Yin

Keyword: Power

Kuan Yin glides through the clouds riding on a dragon. The dragon's head symbolizes her magical powers, which help her to free people from suffering. Her hands are lifted to protect against evil forces.

In Chinese culture, the dragon is a lucky animal. In fact, it is the king of the animals and represents wisdom, strength, transformation, and deep spirituality. Like Kuan Yin, the dragon can move in the sky, in the water, and on earth, transforming as required and undetected in the world of humans. We, too, share some of this ability to transform; for example, we change into the appropriate attire for our professions or for social occasions. This principle of self-transformation applies to our mental and emotional lives as well. In certain situations, we may change internally into unconscious and weak beings, allowing ourselves to be trapped, forgetting that we are in fact powerful dragons.

There is a Chinese legend about a dragon emperor who connects with Kuan Yin through gratitude when the goddess saves his son. His son had changed himself into a fish and was soon caught by fishermen who wanted to sell him at the market. But Kuan Yin freed him, and the grateful emperor rewarded her with a luminescent pearl. The emperor's granddaughter, Lung Nu, brought the pearl to Kuan Yin and became so fascinated by her that she chose to become her disciple.

Contemplation Turn to Dragonhead Kuan Yin when you want to escape from the prison of your thoughts and emotions. Ask her to free you, so you can regain your (dragon) power and open yourself to your true potential.

2

Kuan Yin of Non-Duality

Keyword: Clarification

With her legs crossed in the lotus posture, Kuan Yin sits on a rock holding a golden scepter (also called a *vajra*) in her hands. She wields it as protection from negative energies and demons. In this form, she permits neither procrastination nor timidity, and protects sentient beings from attacks and conflicts.

In Asian traditions, demons are regarded as independent and evil entities that may cause natural disasters, as well as irritations and obsessions within the human mind. There are many Asian ceremonies that use symbolic thrusting weapons to fight demons. Kuan Yin of Non-Duality holds her double-edged scepter for this purpose.

If we hold on to irritations and obsessions, our old mental patterns, we get stuck. Not only do we fail to make progress, we may also become aggressive or depressed. Once caught in these patterns, we tend to develop extreme black-and-white thinking. Instead, we need to find our way back to a balanced center. From the center we can realize that, ultimately, everything is one, and there is no duality. Whenever we succeed in internalizing this point of view, we can enjoy a state of serenity.

> *If they need a vajra-bearing god, he will appear as a*
> *vajra-bearing god and preach the Law for them.*

THE LOTUS SUTRA, CHAPTER 25

Contemplation   Connect with Kuan Yin of Non-Duality if you desire mental clarification or want to banish disturbing thoughts or inner conflicts. Select a personal symbol or visualize Kuan Yin's scepter, and use it to rid yourself of these irritations. Practice relaxation or meditation methods that help you experience non-duality.

3

Kuan Yin of Unity

Keyword: Harmony

As a master of natural energies, Kuan Yin flies through the air, creating thunderstorms and rain for an abundant harvest. At the same time, she comes to the aid of living beings who have been caught in a storm; she can put a stop to the powers of nature at her will. Her right hand, with her thumb and middle finger touching, forms the mudra of unity—in her view, everything is one and all beings are equal.

More and more, we modern humans are withdrawing from nature. We counter the earth's natural powers with highly developed technologies, from lightning rods to dams, creating man-made structures for our protection. But heavy storms, floods, and other natural disasters demonstrate to us that we cannot really dissociate ourselves from nature. Humanity is and will remain a part of the natural world. It is not possible to draw a dividing line between ourselves and nature at any level—physical, mental, or emotional. Once we recognize this principle, we gain insight that leads us to consciously support harmony with nature and with all people through our thoughts, emotions, and actions.

If clouds should bring thunder, and lightning strike,
if hail pelts or drenching rain comes down,
think on the power of that Perceiver of Sounds
and at that moment they will vanish away.

THE LOTUS SUTRA, CHAPTER 25

Contemplation   Call upon Kuan Yin of Unity and ask her to rebalance the turbulence in your environment. As she commands the powers of nature, you may also ask her to protect you during a thunderstorm. Remember that a "thunderstorm" may take the form of a heated discussion or argument that can serve to dissipate tension, leaving you feeling closer to the people in your life.

Kuan Yin of Prayer

Keyword: Devotion

Kuan Yin sits on a huge lotus flower and has placed her palms together for prayer. She connects with all sentient beings and the buddhas in a loving and compassionate way.

Kuan Yin of Prayer appears to those who want to renounce the mundane and devote themselves to their personal spiritual practice. We see in her a spiritual master and teacher who will support us in our personal meditations. By developing our own devotion and compassion, we can enter into her spiritual space and immerse ourselves in her bodhisattva energy.

The Bodhisattva Perceiver of the World's Sounds possesses great authority and supernatural powers . . . and can confer many benefits. For this reason, living beings should constantly keep the thought of him in mind.

THE LOTUS SUTRA, CHAPTER 25

Contemplation   Invoke Kuan Yin of Prayer to deepen your devotion in your meditations. Follow her example: put your palms together, take a few deep breaths, and focus your awareness on your heart. If you can, do this practice near water—at the seashore or on the bank of a river or stream.

Kuan Yin with the Lotus

Keyword: Integrity

Kuan Yin stands on a lotus leaf and holds a beautiful lotus flower. It represents the bodhisattva vow she took to help the sentient beings of all the different worlds, in all the realms of existence, on their path toward enlightenment. The lotus reminds us that she chose to take on this overwhelming task and that she faces it with an unshakeable attitude.

The lotus is also a symbol of purity, wisdom, and enlightenment, as it rises from the murky swamp and unfolds its pure blossom above the water. This corresponds to the path we follow when we strive for realization and liberation.

In the human world, we take vows and make promises that we must observe. For example, we may vow to eat more healthful foods or be more supportive of others. If we fail to stay on this chosen path, great tensions can arise, and we may become estranged from our most cherished goals.

> *Listen to the actions of the Perceiver of Sounds,*
> *how aptly he responds in various quarters.*
> *His vast oath is deep as the ocean . . .*
>
> THE LOTUS SUTRA, CHAPTER 25

Contemplation   Call upon Kuan Yin with the Lotus, and ask her to provide you with clarity about your personal integrity. Examine the promises you have made to yourself and to others and contemplate whether you are—like Kuan Yin—fully committed to what you have sworn. In some cases, it might be best to rethink your promises and formulate them anew, so that you will again be able to follow your spiritual path, the path of the lotus, wholeheartedly.

6

Kuan Yin of Pure Water

Keyword: Blessings

Here we see Kuan Yin floating across the clouds, holding a jeweled bowl filled with pure water in her left hand and a willow twig, which she has dipped into the water, in her right. Sprinkling the earth below her, she provides the land with dew and rain in times of drought, relieving the suffering people who call upon her. Her bowl may also contain medicine to help heal needy beings at all levels of consciousness.

Here Kuan Yin offers us purifying water during difficult times. At a Chinese temple, the priest will often bless the Kuan Yin figurines that her devotees bring to him by taking a willow twig, dipping it into water, and sprinkling the water over them.

Water is the most precious element, sustenance for plants and all other living beings. In Asia it is considered a symbol of prosperity. Feng Shui, the ancient Chinese art of bringing harmony and balance to one's environment, emphasizes the right placement of water features in a house or garden to enhance the occupants' prosperity. The Chinese word for prosperity is itself connected to water; it consists of two characters: on the left is a person dancing joyfully, and on the right is a character that contains the three elements that were important for attaining prosperity in ancient times—water, the sun, and a field.

If living beings encounter weariness or peril,
immeasurable suffering pressing them down,
the power of the Perceiver of Sounds' wonderful wisdom
can save them from the sufferings of the world.

THE LOTUS SUTRA, CHAPTER 25

Contemplation Connect with Kuan Yin of Pure Water, and ask her to quench your thirst and bless you with her waters. Imagine her blessing your drinks, whether you are at home or traveling, charging them with the balancing energies of healing and compassion.

Mother Kuan Yin

Keyword: Love

Paying great respect to all beings, Kuan Yin clasps her palms together and holds a long-stemmed lotus between them. The radiant light emanating from her eyes carries the compassion of the loving mother.

When a mother is in touch with her child, the mighty powers of love and compassion manifest. Her eyes shine as she looks at the child, and she accompanies it patiently and calmly on its path through life. When she and the child have a harmonious relationship, they nurture one another.

He of the true gaze, the pure gaze,
the gaze of great and encompassing wisdom,
the gaze of pity, the gaze of compassion—
constantly we implore him, constantly look up in reverence.

THE LOTUS SUTRA, CHAPTER 25

Contemplation   Whenever you feel sick or abandoned, call upon Mother Kuan Yin, and let yourself bathe in her radiant light. Her energy of unconditional love and service, and the simple fact of her presence, will help you to feel accepted, cared for, and loved again.

Kuan Yin of the Seashell

Keyword: Realization / Insight

Kuan Yin sits before an open shell in which she has been hiding. Her right hand is held in the mudra of unity.

In this form, Kuan Yin watches over sentient beings who are in danger of being harmed by another. So intent is she upon this task that she may even physically manifest as a figurine in order to teach people to be more compassionate. She calls upon us to refrain from exploiting others, and steps from seclusion into the light when we engage in thoughtless or selfish behavior.

A Chinese legend tells of a Tang dynasty emperor whose favorite dish was mussels. He ate large quantities of them. Diving for mussels was dangerous, and in trying to bring him this delicacy some people even paid with their lives. Once when the emperor was eating mussels he found a very large one, which he greedily opened. To his great surprise it contained a tiny statue of Kuan Yin. He bowed deeply before her, burned incense, and had a temple erected for her. From that day on he no longer craved mussels.

Contemplation   Invoke Kuan Yin of the Seashell when you want to open the mussel of realization and break your hard shell of unconsciousness or inconsiderate action. In this way your love and compassion can manifest.

Kuan Yin of Fearlessness

Keyword: Courage

The four-armed Kuan Yin rides on a white lion with her third eye activated. The lion represents the magnificent power of the Buddhist teachings, and his roar symbolizes the truth. In her right front hand she holds the white lotus of truth, in her left front hand a red triple-headed phoenix representing the fire of the South. In her right back hand she holds a small white bird to chase away the darkness, while in her left back hand she carries a fish, whose ever-open eyes represent compassion.

Kuan Yin of Fearlessness blesses all beings and transmits a deep serenity that reaches beyond fear. It is in this active form that she is said to have visited the hells to free the sentient beings there. The hell worlds then became a paradise for a short period of time until Yama, the emperor of hell, asked Kuan Yin to leave.

For this reason you and the others should single-mindedly offer alms to Bodhisattva Perceiver of the World's Sounds who can bestow fearlessness on those who are in fearful, pressing or difficult circumstances. That is why in this saha world everyone calls him Bestower of Fearlessness.

THE LOTUS SUTRA, CHAPTER 25

Contemplation   When you want to be courageous and radiant and kick yourself out of your personal hell of fear, ask Kuan Yin of Fearlessness. Which symbols do you want to carry when confronting your greatest fears and shadows? When you are filled with light, darkness cannot affect you—in fact, you will be banned from the dark world. You may choose to use the symbol of the phoenix, which eternally renews itself and rises from the ashes.

Kuan Yin of the Sutras

Keyword: Impermanence

In her right hand Kuan Yin holds a scroll containing sacred sutra texts. In her left is a stick topped with a skull, representing impermanence and transformation.

The skull that Kuan Yin carries is part of her mortal remains from the lifetime when she was the wife of Malang. It is a reminder of the ephemeral nature of mundane life—that it was only her physical form that died. By following the spiritual practice symbolized by the sutra texts and by practicing devotion, we may connect with eternity. The sacred sutras can positively affect our spirits over a period of many lives.

According to a Chinese legend, during the Tang dynasty there was a beautiful young woman who wanted to marry a man who could recite by heart the Lotus Sutra's chapter about Avalokiteshvara. Several candidates mastered this test. The young woman then asked to hear the complete Lotus Sutra, and gave her suitors just three days to memorize it. A young man called Malang fulfilled her wish and became her bridegroom. But during their wedding night she fell sick and died. Some time later a monk appeared and asked to have her coffin opened. Inside it were bones made of pure gold—a sign of a holy being.

Contemplation   Invoke Kuan Yin of the Sutras, and ask her to provide you with deeper insights into the dual powers of impermanence and eternity. Ask her for support when you want to learn a prayer or another spiritual text by heart.

Kuan Yin of the Rock Cave

Keyword: Detoxification

Kuan Yin sits at the entrance to a rock cave in the royal—also called the "royal ease"—pose. Poisonous animals, as well as the energies of diseases, gather at this spot. But she eliminates them, using the mysterious powers she possesses to protect sentient beings.

As modern towns and cities have grown, the threat of poisonous animals has been reduced in many countries, as they have been deprived of their habitats. But now we are exposed to numerous toxic substances—those caused by exhaust fumes or accidents at chemical or nuclear power plants, for example. And we humans carry harmful toxins inside us as well, on both the physical and mental levels. Chinese medicine describes the five "hollow (cavelike) organs" where toxins accumulate. Buddhism describes three "mental poisons" that cause disease and act as obstacles on the path toward enlightenment: greed, hatred, and ignorance.

If lizards, snakes, vipers, scorpions
threaten you with poison breath that sears like flame,
think on the power of that Perceiver of Sounds
and, hearing your voice, they will flee of themselves.

THE LOTUS SUTRA, CHAPTER 25

Contemplation   Invoke Kuan Yin of the Rock Cave when you want to clear your physical, mental, and emotional "secret caves" from poisons and unresolved feelings. Tune in to her when you want to detoxify or work on dissolving negative or stressful emotions and thoughts.

Kuan Yin of Universal Compassion

Keyword: Mercy

Kuan Yin stands on a mountain, holding the nectar vase in her left hand and the essence pearl in her right. She is deeply touched by the suffering of all beings and distributes her universal compassion to every one of them—because in her view they are all equal.

Kuan Yin's river of mercy reaches not only the sentient beings on our earth, but the whole universe. Those who devote themselves with bountiful trust may achieve liberation. Devotion and trust must, however, be truly experienced and originate from our hearts; they are of no use if we use them rationally as strategic "tools." We are asked to actively practice compassion by supporting others. When we fulfill our tasks in this world, we must not look at them as our personal achievements, but as contributions to the benefit of everyone.

> *Perceiver of the World's Sounds, pure sage—*
> *to those in suffering, in danger of death,*
> *he can offer aid and support.*
> *Endowed with all benefits,*
> *he views living beings with compassionate eyes.*

FROM THE LOTUS SUTRA, CHAPTER 25

Contemplation   Tune in to Kuan Yin of Universal Compassion when you consider your work and actions in this world, so that you may deepen them. Recognize the ways in which you devote yourself to the universal stream of mercy, thereby gaining energy and trust.

13

Kuan Yin of the Six Time Periods

Keyword: Time

Standing on a hill, Kuan Yin holds a sutra scroll. Her right hand is in the gesture of granting a wish: the palm faces forward and the fingers point down. According to ancient Indian and Chinese cosmology, day and night can be subdivided into six double hours each. Kuan Yin of the Six Time Periods protects us at all times of day and night.

Observations and studies of the cosmic cycles are as old as humanity. People have researched these rhythms in order to make use of their powers. Whether farmer or businessperson, everyone wants to know which moment is auspicious for a certain activity. In Asia, various systems serve this purpose. According to an ancient Asian tradition, there are six goddesses of time, each of them ruling a powerful period, such as sunrise or sunset. Chinese astrology uses the system of the double hours for day and night, attributing special elements and zodiac signs, and thus specific qualities, to them. Kuan Yin knows and respects the time cycles of this world, but ultimately transcends them because she acts from the realm of eternity.

> *He is endowed with transcendental powers*
> *and widely practices the expedient means of wisdom.*
> *Throughout the lands in the ten directions*
> *there is no region where he does not manifest himself.*

THE LOTUS SUTRA, CHAPTER 25

Contemplation   Get in touch with Kuan Yin of the Six Time Periods if you want to find an auspicious time for an important event. Be aware that you will always be able to tap in to her energy.

14

Kuan Yin of Serenity

Keyword: Anchoring / Grounding

Suan Yin sits on a small rock amid the ocean surf. She has put her palms together and rests in deep contemplation. In this form, she protects sentient beings who are the victims of disaster or those who are at death's door.

When we experience a disaster or bad luck, we become disoriented. We feel helpless in the face of the situation and lose sight of our path. Fundamentally, we humans are subject to our emotions and instincts and travel the cycle of rebirths without gaining a greater overview. Usually we become even more confused as we approach death, reluctant to leave this world.

If they have great wrath and ire, let them think with constant reverence of Bodhisattva Perceiver of the World's Sounds and then they can shed their ire. If they have great ignorance and stupidity, let them think with constant reverence of Bodhisattva Perceiver of the World's Sounds and they can rid themselves of stupidity.

THE LOTUS SUTRA, CHAPTER 26

Contemplation Connect with Kuan Yin of Serenity when your sight is blurred by emotion and you have lost your bearings. In this painting she is as firm as a rock and looks fully centered. You may tune in to her, re-anchor within yourself, and find peace—no matter how high the waves.

15

Kuan Yin of Joy

Keyword: Happiness

Kuan Yin sits upon clouds in the royal pose, offering her gentle compassion and her smile. She imparts the spiritual teachings with joy and happiness. In this form, Kuan Yin also protects seekers who are moving toward the peak of realization.

Here Kuan Yin appeals to us to adapt a playful and joyful attitude. Even if we have gone far in life, experienced many falls, and had to start anew, we should—like a child who tirelessly struggles to learn to walk—get up, laugh, and start all over again. On the mundane level of suffering, we are carried by Kuan Yin's compassion, and on the spiritual level we can recognize life as the cosmic game it is—and burst into relieved laughter. The combination of serenity and humor loosens the chains of seriousness and our identification with the limitations of ordinary life, and we can face our challenges with calm and ease.

Suppose you are on the peak of Mount Sumeru
and someone pushes you off.
Think on the power of that Perceiver of Sounds
and you will hang in midair like the sun!
Suppose you are pursued by evil men
who wish to throw you down from a diamond mountain.
Think on the power of that Perceiver of Sounds
and they cannot harm a hair of you!

THE LOTUS SUTRA, CHAPTER 25

Contemplation Get in touch with Kuan Yin of Joy when the serious side of life is weighing heavily upon you. Let yourself be inspired by her soft, serene smile, and smile to yourself once again. In this way you can reconnect to the lightness of being. Focus your attention on those areas in your life that are most cheerful and effortless.

Kuan Yin of Treasures

Keyword: Prosperity

Kuan Yin sits upon a rock. Her right hand touches its surface, while her left arm rests upon her knee. Her pose is relaxed and peaceful. In this form, she protects treasure hunters who have lost their way at sea and are prone to falling prey to evil forces.

On the worldly level, we all strive for prosperity; everyone has to secure a livelihood, and it is not wrong to enjoy mundane riches. However, if we strive exclusively for these possessions, in the long run we will become exhausted and dissatisfied.

Kuan Yin not only protects us during our search for earthly treasures, she also prevents us from getting lost and falling prey to negative forces. Ultimately, we can also gain spiritual treasures in life. Further, she sends us the precious message that the most valuable treasure is not to be found outside, but deeply within ourselves.

Suppose there were a hundred, a thousand, ten thousand, a million living beings who, seeking for gold, silver, lapis lazuli, seashell, agate, coral, amber, pearls, and other treasures, set out on the great sea. And suppose a fierce wind should blow their ship off course and it drifted to the land of rakshasas demons. If among those people there is even just one who calls the name of Bodhisattva Perceiver of the World's Sounds, then all those people will be delivered from their troubles with the rakshasas.

THE LOTUS SUTRA, CHAPTER 25

Contemplation   Open yourself to Kuan Yin of Treasures when you notice that you have lost your sense of inner abundance and you feel empty and exhausted. She can help you to reorient yourself and create worldly goals without neglecting your spiritual practice. Get to know your greatest treasure in life.

Longevity Kuan Yin

Keyword: Safety

Adorned with a magnificent peacock-feather crown containing the image of Buddha Amitabha, Kuan Yin reaches out with her sixteen radial arms. Two hands rest in her lap in a meditation pose while another pair of hands is joined in prayer. In this manifestation, Kuan Yin protects sentient beings from attacks by their enemies and prolongs lives.

With her multiple arms, Kuan Yin can act and protect on many levels at once. The number of arms shown in this image is merely symbolic, as her countless hands and eyes support all sentient beings at all times. In this form, she acts as a guardian angel, helping many people at once.

Sometimes we, too, wish we had many arms in order to fulfill all the tasks that life presents to us. Often, we seek safety and relaxation in life. But Kuan Yin reaches beyond those goals and intervenes at subtle, spiritual levels—thus preventing dangers and catastrophes.

Suppose with curses and various poisonous herbs
someone should try to injure you.
Think on the power of that Perceiver of Sounds
and the injury will rebound upon the originator.

THE LOTUS SUTRA, CHAPTER 26

Contemplation   Get in touch with Longevity Kuan Yin, who coordinates and masters the cosmic processes, in order to make your life smoother at all levels of consciousness. Ask her to dissolve your obstacles more quickly so that you can understand the message of life at this very moment and contribute to your growth. Visualize yourself as the thousand-armed bodhisattva who is able to support a large number of beings simultaneously.

Kuan Yin with the Blue Neck

Keyword: Transformation

Kuan Yin sits at the seashore. In her left hand she holds a beautiful lotus, while her right hand forms the wish-fulfilling mudra. Her face and neck have a blue shimmer—because she has drunk poison! In this form, she protects sentient beings from poisoning and disease and liberates them from karma.

According to Chinese legend, Kuan Yin drank a poison that arose from the ocean and could have killed all of the sentient beings in the world. In this way, she symbolically cleansed the delusions and misdeeds of beings at all levels of consciousness.

This story resembles that of the Indian god Shiva, who saved the world by collecting in a vial poison that rose from the sea. Because he could not dispose of it anywhere without exposing all beings to its deadly danger, he drank it. Shiva's face and neck also turned blue, but he transformed the poison.

In this image we see Kuan Yin literally swallowing our wrong deeds, aberrations, and mental poisons to prevent our downfall.

Suppose you encounter evil rakshasas,
poison dragons and various demons.
Think on the power of that Perceiver of Sounds
and then none of them will dare to harm you.

THE LOTUS SUTRA, CHAPTER 25

Contemplation Turn to Kuan Yin with the Blue Neck to free yourself from burdens caused by disease and toxic substances, as well as harmful beings. Examine how you can stimulate the self-healing powers of your body and mind to prevent rigidity and the accumulation of harmful residues.

19

One-Leaf Kuan Yin

Keyword: Consciousness

Here we see Kuan Yin standing on a lotus petal, gliding across the ocean. In her left hand she holds a jade Joo-I scepter, symbol of the Buddhist teachings, and in her right the essence pearl, the "wish-fulfilling jewel." In this form, she protects us from premature death and the dangers of water.

A legend tells of a Japanese monk who had studied Buddhism in China and wanted to return to Japan. His boat was caught in a storm and he started to pray. Suddenly he saw Kuan Yin gliding on a lotus petal across the waves. At that very moment the storm calmed, and the boat was saved.

Another version of this legend tells that the monk had stolen a Kuan Yin figurine and taken it aboard the boat. Kuan Yin appeared to him as well, but to point out his greed.

In this image Kuan Yin appears as "cosmic surfer" who will maintain her clarity and consciousness even during the greatest turbulence. She shows us the way when we are overwhelmed by the unconsciousness of worldly life and need support and reorientation.

If one were washed away by a great flood and called upon his name,
one would immediately find himself in a shallow place.

THE LOTUS SUTRA, CHAPTER 26

Contemplation   Invoke One-Leaf Kuan Yin if you are in danger of being overwhelmed by waves of unconsciousness; use her consciousness-supporting power and her skill to traverse those seas. Imagine yourself skillfully surfing across the roiling seas on your personal lotus petal—your wisdom and self-realization.

20

Water-Moon Kuan Yin

Keyword: Reflection

With the full moon reflecting on the water, Kuan Yin stands on a lotus flower atop a pedestal of rock. In her left hand she holds a lotus flower, while from the vase in her right hand she pours the crystal-clear nectar of compassion.

According to a Chinese saying: "The one moon reflects in one thousand rivers, and all one thousand rivers reflect the one moon. One spring nourishes countless flowers, and myriad flowers breathe the miracle of the one spring."

Ultimately, there is no difference between buddhas, bodhisattvas, and humans. Man, too, owns the Buddha nature, although he is not yet conscious of the nature of reality. Only through enlightenment will he become a buddha.

According to Chinese cosmology, he will first enter the trinity of "heaven-human-earth" and then the One—the Tao. In Tao there is no more separation—man himself may become Kuan Yin.

He sends down the sweet dew, the Dharma rain,
to quench the flames of earthly desires.

THE LOTUS SUTRA, CHAPTER 26

Contemplation   Connect with Water-Moon Kuan Yin if you want to further examine what the world is reflecting to you. Find out where you can touch its essence directly, instead of falling for its mirror image. Water-Moon Kuan Yin can support you in gaining deeper insight into the principle of cause and effect.

Kuan Yin with the Fish Basket
Keyword: Life

Here Kuan Yin appears as a young woman. She walks on the beach, carrying a bamboo basket filled with fish. Their ever-open eyes represent the eyes of compassion. Fish are also a symbol of prosperity and abundance.

Buddhism teaches that releasing animals that have been caught creates great blessings and prolongs one's life. We should not focus solely on our own self-interest, because this will not create genuine prosperity. If, instead, we compassionately share our environment with others and support them, everyone will experience great abundance. This is a way to create protective and connecting bridges between us.

In a Chinese legend, Kuan Yin appears as the girl Ling-chao, who sells fish. A strong bridge for protection from flooding is to be built from her profits. But Ling-chao has a requirement: people who buy her fish are not to kill them, but instead must release them back into the sea.

Contemplation   Tune in to Kuan Yin with the Fish Basket when you want to experience the web of life, so that you may be more respectful of it and to make your own positive contribution to it. Check for things in your home that you are not using, and donate them for a worthy purpose.

22

Waterfall Kuan Yin

Keyword: Regeneration

Kuan Yin sits beside a waterfall, listening to the rushing torrent of water. In this form, she protects sentient beings from the dangers of fire.

Water is one of the most important elements of life. This image does not represent its potential dangers; on the contrary, it might save our lives. In the form of a waterfall, water displays its refreshing, healing effects and activates its environment. As it moves along its natural paths, across rocks and through varied landscapes, it humidifies the air and calms us with its many sounds.

The fire from which Kuan Yin protects us is harmful; it represents emotions such as hatred, envy, and anxiety. These may actually create acids similar to fire in our bodies; we may fall into a "pit of fire." Waterfall Kuan Yin fills this pit with healing water, helping us to regenerate and gain strength.

Suppose someone should conceive a wish to harm you,
should push you into a great pit of fire.
Think on the power of that Perceiver of Sounds
and the pit of fire will change into a pond!

THE LOTUS SUTRA, CHAPTER 25

Contemplation   Turn to Waterfall Kuan Yin if you perceive a destructive fire within you or around you. Choose a meditation place that is near water, and listen to its relaxing sounds.

23

Medicine Kuan Yin

Keyword: Health

Kuan Yin has placed her right hand into her left and carries the vase that holds the healing nectar of compassion. During times of disease or epidemic, she gives us health and optimism.

In ancient times, people asked Kuan Yin for help in difficult situations. When she granted healing, they collected money so they could honor her by building temples. During Kuan Yin ceremonies, the people frequently put bottles of water next to the altar and distributed it to everyone at the end of the service. This water was said to have healing powers, as it had been energized by the vibrations of the invocations and mantras practiced there.

> *In many different kinds of evil circumstances,*
> *in the realms of hell, hungry spirits or beasts,*
> *the sufferings of birth, old age, sickness and death—*
> *all these he bit by bit wipes out.*

THE LOTUS SUTRA, CHAPTER 26

Contemplation   Open yourself to Medicine Kuan Yin if you want to strengthen or regain your health. You can also hold your medicine or a cup of water and visualize Kuan Yin charging it with pure vibrations.

24

White-Robed Kuan Yin

Keyword: Peace

Standing upon a magnificent white lotus, Kuan Yin holds another white lotus flower in her left hand. She wears flowing white robes and a veil and holds her right hand in the mudra of fearlessness. In this form, Kuan Yin grants peace and hears the prayers of the people.

The color white represents purity, merit, and the enlightened spirit. We feel better and more pure if we have "put our house in order" and carry no deadwood. We also develop purity through devotion and merit—through serving others. This is easier if we are not busy working on our own issues, when we have made peace with ourselves.

> *Endowed with all benefits,*
> *he views living beings with compassionate eyes.*
> *The sea of his accumulated blessings is immeasurable;*
> *therefore you should bow your head to him!*

THE LOTUS SUTRA, CHAPTER 25

Contemplation   Tune in to White-Robed Kuan Yin if you wish to have more peace in your life, and if you would like to enjoy more inspiration and ease on your personal path to enlightenment.

Kuan Yin with the Willow Branch

Keyword: Flexibility

In this image, Kuan Yin sits upon a rock. She rests her left hand upon her cheek, indicating her contemplative state. Her right hand holds the willow branch that she uses to sprinkle water and the nectar of compassion. Kuan Yin with the Willow Branch is also associated with the Indian god Brahma, the creator who rules the world of forms.

The willow is known for its flexibility; its branches are so pliable that they can be used for weaving. The willow tree also contains valuable substances that can be used for medical treatment. Here, the willow represents Kuan Yin's ability to manifest in countless appearances and to adapt to the respective states of mind of the people.

The Lotus Sutra compares the voice of Brahma or Kuan Yin with the sound of the ocean surf—a cosmic primordial tone that we can perceive at any time once we have tuned in to it.

> *Wonderful sound, Perceiver of the World's Sounds,*
> *Brahma's sound, the sea tide sound—*
> *they surpass those sounds of the world;*
> *therefore you should constantly think on them*
> *from thought to thought never entertaining doubt!*

THE LOTUS SUTRA, CHAPTER 25

Contemplation If you find yourself paralyzed—no matter on what level—contemplate Kuan Yin with the Willow Branch, and ask her to support your flexibility, openness, and adaptability. Sit in a quiet place or near water, and listen for the voice of Kuan Yin. When you can hear this sound, you will experience that the whole of creation is one, and there is no separation.

26

Four-Armed Kuan Yin

Keyword: Protective Shield

Four-Armed Kuan Yin holds grapes in her front right hand, a symbol of growth and a good harvest. In her left front hand she carries an axe, countering evil forces and protecting sentient beings from oppression. Her back right hand shows the wish-fulfilling mudra while her back left hand holds a rope that can bind all kinds of adversities. In this form, Kuan Yin protects from enemy attacks.

A Chinese legend tells of a prisoner who had been sentenced to death, although he was innocent of any crime. The night before he was to be executed, he dreamed that he was visited by a Buddhist monk who taught him a sutra text. The sentenced man recited this sutra one hundred times. The next morning, when the executioner tried to put him to death, three of his swords broke into pieces. In respect for the mysterious powers protecting his life, the prisoner was released. When the man returned home, he discovered that the Kuan Yin picture on his altar appeared to have been cut by three strokes of a sword.

Suppose you encounter trouble with the king's law,
face punishment, about to forfeit your life.
Think on the power of that Perceiver of Sounds
and the executioner's sword will be broken to bits!

THE LOTUS SUTRA, CHAPTER 25

Contemplation Call upon Four-Armed Kuan Yin if you need special protection during difficult times. Receive her nourishing energy, so you may continue to grow under her protection.

27

Anu Kuan Yin

Keyword: Sanctuary

Seated on a rock surrounded by water, Kuan Yin looks over an expansive sacred lake. Her presence blesses all beings living nearby, and she provides protection from the perils of the swirling water.

Anu is considered the manifestation of a crystal-clear sacred lake that, according to Indian legend, is located on the northern side of the Himalayas. Four sacred rivers flow from this lake. Its shores are covered in gold, silver, and emeralds, and the beaches are golden sand.

The holy lake Anu is a special power spot. Here, everything is purified, and this is the energy Kuan Yin represents. The water (mind) is crystal clear; there are no clouds or disturbances. Gold and silver represent the universal energies, and emeralds stand for communication, spiritual powers, and the energy of the heart. The four sacred rivers spread out to the four directions, carrying the pure, sacred consciousness of Kuan Yin throughout the world.

If there are living beings who hear this chapter on Bodhisattva Perceiver of the World's Sounds, on the freedom of his actions, his manifestation of a universal gateway, and his transcendental powers, it should be known that the benefits these persons gain are not few!

THE LOTUS SUTRA, CHAPTER 25

Contemplation   Open yourself to Anu Kuan Yin if you wish to be purified and access your inner sanctuary. Visualize this sanctuary, and explore how you would like to use it.

28

Kuan Yin with a Halo of Fire

Keyword: Light

Kuan Yin sits upon a rock, surrounded by a ring of flames. Her right hand forms the mudra of teaching. The purging, sacred fire represents Kuan Yin's powerful action, banning natural disasters and all kinds of other dangers. Her radiant light illuminates the world, filling it with wisdom and peace.

Fire in this form has a cleansing effect, driving away darkness and revealing purity and wisdom. Light has incredible power and acts as an all-penetrating spark of life (*Qi* in Chinese, *prana* in Sanskrit), eliminating all negative forces. Kuan Yin appears here in her so-called "wrathful aspect," indicated by the ring of fire. She is the powerful protectress who will destroy or burn if necessary in order to pave the way toward enlightenment. But her action is not driven by anger—an emotion also attributed to fiery qualities. Instead, Kuan Yin is motivated by her deepest compassion.

His pure light, free of blemish,
is a sun of wisdom dispelling all darknesses.
He can quell the wind and fire of misfortune
and everywhere bring light to the world.

THE LOTUS SUTRA, CHAPTER 25

Contemplation   Tune in to Kuan Yin with a Halo of Fire if you want to illuminate dark corners of your life or mind. See her purifying anything negative you find there with her cosmic fire.

29

Kuan Yin of Virtue

Keyword: Single-mindedness

Kuan Yin sits upon a rock, holding a golden scepter studded with gemstones in her left hand and a lotus flower in her right. In this form, she appears as a heavenly general with majestic powers to whom the sentient beings pay respect.

The heavenly general is also named Vaishravana—"the one who hears everything." Radiating the virtue of a compassionate warrior, Kuan Yin reflects the power and devotion of an advocate who strives for higher aims.

Frequently, we humans are so entangled in our everyday battles, with all of their petty issues, that we lose sight of the higher goals we would like to achieve. When we regain our focus and our vision, we can go out into the world like a heavenly general and powerfully tackle the tasks before us.

> *When law suits bring you before the officials,*
> *when terrified in the midst of an army,*
> *think on the power of that Perceiver of Sounds*
> *and hatred in all its forms will be dispelled.*

THE LOTUS SUTRA, CHAPTER 25

Contemplation   Get in touch with Kuan Yin of Virtue if you wish to clarify what you envision for yourself and concentrate more intently on your goals. Listen within, and learn what you really need to do.

30

Leaf-Robed Kuan Yin

Keyword: Centering

Wearing a robe made of leaves, Kuan Yin sits in contemplation atop the peak of the sacred mountain Sumeru. She hides both hands in her sleeves. In this form, she is compared with the Indian god Shakra, or Indra, who masters the forces of nature and also resides on Mount Sumeru. In this manifestation, Kuan Yin protects us from diseases, epidemics, and insects, prolongs life, and wards off evil.

Plants are important servants to humanity: they can be our food, building material, or medicine. The plant kingdom blankets the earth and helps to purify it; plant materials clothe us as well. Here, Kuan Yin's leaf robe represents a passive shield from pestilence and disturbing insects—and she has selected a very special remote place in nature to dwell. According to Buddhism, Mount Sumeru is a powerful spot at the center of the universe. As a silent observer, she sits exactly at the intersection of all the realms of the cosmos, but is always ready to support sentient beings.

If they need the lord Shakra to be saved, immediately he becomes the lord Shakra and preaches the Law for them.

THE LOTUS SUTRA, CHAPTER 25

Contemplation   Tune in to Leaf-robed Kuan Yin when you want to use her nourishing and empowering energy of concentration. Remember the power of retreat to reconnect you with your vital energy. Choose clothing in colors and textures that protect you and make you feel happy.

31

Kuan Yin on a Lotus Leaf

Keyword: Faith

In a relaxed but regal pose, Kuan Yin sits on a lotus leaf. Faith and devotion are important aspects of the human belief system.

A Chinese legend tells of a businessman to whom Kuan Yin appears in a dream. She gives him a detailed description of where to find a statue of her. The businessman takes this dream seriously and, shortly afterward, finds the statue on a lotus leaf along the riverbank.

A similar story describes a man trying to fix a Kuan Yin statue he has found on a carved lotus-shaped pedestal. But the small figurine is so severely damaged that he has to install it on the pedestal in a horizontal position; still, he honors this manifestation of Kuan Yin.

In both legends a man has a dream or a divine vision and does what he has been asked to do. Both times he finds a material form of Kuan Yin that he treats respectfully and that in return supports his faith.

I will describe him in outline for you—
listen to his name, observe his body,
bear him in mind, not passing the time vainly,
for he can wipe out the pains of existence.

THE LOTUS SUTRA, CHAPTER 25

Contemplation   Connect with Kuan Yin on a Lotus Leaf if you want a hint about what you need to do to reach your goals. Ask her to guide you in your dreams or during a vision quest.

Dragonfish Kuan Yin

Keyword: Taming

Kuan Yin stands on the back of a dragonfish as it glides through the sea. Her right hand forms the mudra of teaching, and in her left she holds a golden hook.

This image evokes a Chinese legend about a dragonfish that created havoc in a fishing village on the Southern Sea, destroying boats, coming onto land, even eating humans and animals. Kuan Yin came to the rescue, fighting the fish and taming him by using a golden hook that she had made especially for this purpose. With Kuan Yin on his back, the dragonfish glided back into the water and left the Southern Sea forever. In gratitude, the fishermen built a temple with a statue of Kuan Yin riding the dragonfish.

In this image, nature, with all its unruly forces and perils, appears in the form of a dragonfish, a monster of the sea. As animals' instincts are not fully subdued, and they often react to spiritual energies, Kuan Yin demonstrates how to tame the dragonfish by using a hook: a symbol of spiritual powers. For this purpose, she neither catches him with a fishing rod nor kills him. The dragonfish willingly leaves his hunting ground, and even allows Kuan Yin to ride on his back.

If you should be cast adrift on the vast ocean,
menaced by dragons, fish, and various demons,
think on the power of that Perceiver of Sounds
and the billows and waves cannot drown you!

THE LOTUS SUTRA, CHAPTER 25

Contemplation   Turn to Dragonfish Kuan Yin if you want to let go of your anger and instead manifest gentleness and understanding. You may also invoke her if you meet animals that will not heed you or that react in an aggressive way.

Kuan Yin with Children

Keyword: Creativity

Kuan Yin holds a child in her arms while two other children grasp her robes. In this manifestation, she fulfills the wish for a child and acts as a protectress of pregnant women and mothers.

All cultures appreciate children—they represent the creative potential that will shape the future. A child also expresses the fertility of a couple and continues the family. But our creative power does not manifest only at this physical level. When we commit to projects with full spirit and put our whole hearts into them, they are our mental children, who may also have an impact on the future. Whether through an invention, the founding of an organization, or the focused passing on of precious knowledge—we manifest our creativity and offer considerable benefits to humankind.

If a woman wishes to give birth to a male child, she should offer obeisance and alms to Bodhisattva Perceiver of the World's Sounds and then she will bear a son blessed with merit, virtue, and wisdom. And if she wishes to bear a daughter, she will bear one with all the marks of comeliness, one who in the past planted the roots of virtue and is loved and respected by many persons.

THE LOTUS SUTRA, CHAPTER 25

Contemplation   Invoke Kuan Yin with Children if you want to have a child or wish to have better communication with children. You can also connect with her if you want to powerfully manifest your creative potential.

Connecting with Kuan Yin

 The thirty-three images for contemplation in the preceding chapter have already given you the opportunity to personally connect with Kuan Yin's many forms in your own way. You can meditate on the paintings, passages from the Lotus Sutra, or any other elements that speak to you. This intuitive approach is there to support you whenever you experience a difficult situation, or would simply like to bring Kuan Yin into your day and receive some inspiration.

This chapter will provide additional ways to get in touch with Kuan Yin. I will walk you through mantras, meditations, visualizations, and the process of designing your own Kuan Yin altar. And you will gain new insights into Kuan Yin's enlightenment path—the path of listening. Each of these practices is spiritually nourishing in its own way.

Mantras

Perhaps the simplest way to invoke Kuan Yin is by reciting her mantra. A mantra is a series of meaningful symbols that we repeat in a mindful way. This has a calming effect on the mind; it interrupts our restless thought forms and shifts our focus, empowering us and bringing inner peace. It is not unusual for Kuan Yin to appear to us in visions or dreams that mirror our own situations after we have recited her mantra.

If you need quick help in a trying time, you can invoke Kuan Yin with her mantras alone, without any other ritual or ceremony. If you are not familiar with

the pronunciation but still have a strong desire to chant them aloud, you may do so by respectfully invoking Kuan Yin with strong intention. There are also recordings available of Kuan Yin mantra chants.

— Namo Kuan Shi Yin Pusa —

In this Chinese mantra, we call upon Kuan Yin directly by using her name. Its literal translation is: "I take refuge in Bodhisattva Kuan Shi Yin, who observes the cries of the world." Repeat this mantra, chanting aloud or silently, until a critical situation you are facing has passed, or your mind and heart have eased. This may take just a few minutes—or it may take hours. You can also recite this mantra on behalf of a loved one who is ill. Here is what the syllables mean:

Namo—worship, take refuge
Kuan—observe, perceive
Shi—world
Yin—sound, voice, cry
Pusa—bodhisattva
(pronounced nah moh kwan shih yin poo sah)

A variation of the mantra in English is "I call upon Bodhisattva Kuan Yin, who sees and hears the cries of the world." You can use this mantra to place a ceremony of your own personal design under Kuan Yin's protection, reciting the sentence several times and then making any special request of her that you may have.

Always prepared to help: Kuan Yin equipped with symbolic objects.

— Om Mani Padme Hum —

This is the classic Sanskrit Kuan Yin mantra. The rough translation is "Hail to the jewel in the lotus." Imagine that there is a beautiful lotus flowering in your heart, with Kuan Yin at its center, as you recite it. See Kuan Yin as the jewel emanating a radiant light.

When chanting this mantra, you may choose instead to visualize the male form of Kuan Yin, Avalokiteshvara. According to legend, Buddha Amitabha was reciting *Om Mani Padme Hum* while in a state of ecstasy as Avalokiteshvara was born from a ray of light emanating from his eye.

A Simple Buddhist Kuan Yin Meditation

In this simple but powerful meditation, you gradually increase the tempo of the mantra. Recite or chant *Namo Kuan Shi Yin Pusa* or *Om Mani Padme Hum*, slowly at first and then faster and faster. This creates a rhythmic vibration that intensifies as you chant. Sounding a bell or striking another small percussion instrument will enhance the experience. In the temples, the tone is struck with each syllable, which can be quite challenging as the chant speeds up; you may choose a slower rhythm, perhaps after each recitation of the full mantra, if you wish.

You may practice this meditation while sitting, or slowly walking in a circle—perhaps in your home at your altar or another power spot, or outdoors. After you strike the final percussion tone, return to your meditation seat if you have been walking, and immerse yourself in the silence; it will be very powerful. Make use of this deep stillness, and meditate for a minimum of twenty minutes.

A Kuan Yin Walking Meditation

During this meditation, you will chant *Namo Kuan Shi Yin Pusa* or *Om Mani Padme Hum* while walking in a special way described in ancient legend. You will move as though you are approaching a temple along the staircases and pathways that lead devoted pilgrims toward a Kuan Yin shrine. Sound a bell, take two steps forward, and then prostrate yourself—an expression of penitence, as well as honor and respect for the bodhisattva. Depending on your fitness level, you may either touch the ground with your hands or bow down until your forehead touches it. Your single-minded intention to connect with Kuan Yin is more important than perfecting the body movement. Many pilgrims engage in this practice on the island of Putuo Shan.

The Great Dharani of Compassion

The Great Dharani of Compassion is the long ceremony that I described experiencing at Hsi Lai Temple in the introduction to this book. If you have the opportunity to participate in this ritual, don't pass it up: it is an unforgettable experience.

A dharani is a sequence of sacred syllables. It is similar to a mantra in this way, but significantly longer. The Lotus Sutra refers to a dharani as a "magical sentence," and its recitation usually forms the culmination point of a spiritual ceremony. In this case, the ceremony and the dharani share the same name.

The full name of the Great Dharani of Compassion mantra is "Dharani of the thousand-armed and thousand-eyed Avalokiteshvara Bodhisattva who embraces everything with compassion." It is multifaceted and complex, invoking eighty-four different bodhisattvas. It is also said to describe the forty-two dharani hands of the thousand-armed Avalokiteshvara, each carrying a special symbol.

This three-hour ritual is held regularly at Chinese and Japanese Buddhist temples. Alternating chanting and prostration are followed by reciting the magical dharani sentence several times, while devotees walk in serpentine fashion between rows of prayer cushions. The devout atmosphere creates a strong energy field in which all fuses into one. The ceremony can be simple or more elaborate—including offerings of flowers, rice, and sandalwood. Worshippers may receive a small bottle of spiritually charged water at the end of the ritual.

The Great Dharani of Compassion ceremony has a profound, purifying effect, leaving participants with a wonderful feeling of inner peace. And this is precisely its goal: to cleanse the mind of greed, anger, worry, fear, and illusion.

The Great Dharani is popular all over the world, and with good reason. It promises reincarnation into the higher worlds, respect, strong connections to other people, healthy sensory organs, an abundance of food, prosperity, and the opportunity to study Buddhist teachings. Those who chant the mantra are said to be protected from starvation, disease, poisoning, and natural disasters. It not only improves its practitioners' condition in this life, but also helps them to be reborn in the Pure Land of Buddha Amitabha, where they have the chance to enjoy further teachings that lead toward enlightenment.

This book contains just one Chinese version of the long mantra (opposite page). To fully explore the Dharani would fill yet another book, as there are multiple versions in Chinese, Japanese, and Korean as well as several retranslations into Sanskrit, its original language.

If you want to learn to pronounce this long mantra, it is best to attend the dharani ritual at a temple or purchase a CD. But if you simply open the book to the next page and place it in a positive place in your home or office, its vibrations will begin to radiate into the room. Chanting it is, of course, much more powerful.

It is important to treat the Great Dharani with great respect. You may choose to make it part of a simple meditation that starts with an invocation and an offering of incense.

The Great Dharani of Compassion Mantra

Nan mo he la da na
duo la ye ye
Nan mo a li ye
Po lu jie di
Shuo bo la ye
Pu ti sa duo po ye
Mo he sa duo po ye
Mo he jia lu ni jia ye
An
Sa po la fa yi
Shu da na da xie
Nan mo xi ji li duo yi
meng a li ye
Po lu ji di
Shi fo la neng tuo po
Nan mo na la jin chi
Xi li mo he
Bo duo sha mie
Sa po a ta dou shu peng
A shi yun
Sa po sa duo
Na mo po sa duo
Na mo po jie
Mo fa te dou
Da zhi ta

An
A po lu xi
Lu jia di
Jia luo di
Yi xi li
Mo he pu ti sa duo
Sa po sa po
Mo la mo la
Mo xi mo xi
Li tuo yun
Ju lu ju lu jie mong
Du lu du lu fa she ye di
Mo he fa she ye di
Tuo la tuo la
Di li ni
Shi fo la ye
Zhe la zhe la
mo mo fa mo la
Mu di li
Yi xi yi xi
Shi na shi na
A la seng fo la she li
Fa sa fa seng
Fo la she ye
Hu lu hu lu mo la

Hu lu hu lu xi li
Suo la suo la
Xi li xi li
Su lu su lu
Pu ti ye
Pu ti ye
Pu tuo ye
Pu tuo ye
Mi di li ye
Na la jin chi
Di li se ni na
Po ye mo na
Suo po he
Xi tuo ye
Suo po he
Mo he xi tuo ye
Suo po he
Xi tuo yu yi
Shi po la ye
Suo po he
Na la jin chi
Suo po he
Mo la na la
Suo po he
Xi la seng

A mu jie ye
Suo po he
Suo po mo he a xi tuo ye
Suo po he
Zhe ji la a xi tuo ye
Suo po he
Po tuo mo jie xi tuo ye
Suo po he
Na la jin chi
Po jie la ye
Suo po he
Mo po li sheng jie la ye
Suo po he
Mo po li sheng jie la ye
Suo po he
Nan mo he la da
na duo la ye ye
Nan mo a li ye
Po lu ji di
Shuo po la ye
Suo po he
An xi dian du
Man duo la
Pa tuo ye
Suo po he

Charging the Sacred Waters of Kuan Yin

Here is a simple practice that easily connects you to Kuan Yin's energy. Before you meditate or recite a mantra at your altar, place pure, clean water in a glass or porcelain container (no plastic) in front of a statue or a picture of Kuan Yin. The longer and more intense your spiritual practice at your altar, the more powerfully this water will be charged with protective spiritual energy. You may drink it immediately afterward or apply it to an area of your body that you would like to bring into balance. You may also place some tumbled stones, such as rose quartz, jade, or quartz crystal, in the water, or add a bit of top-quality natural rose water. Pour any remaining water into a bottle and seal it tightly. Store it in a cool place and consume it within three days, or sprinkle this potent Kuan Yin water in your garden or another favorite place outdoors.

Visualizations

Following are several visualizations to help you tune in to Kuan Yin. You may do them by themselves, or combine them with other meditation practices, if you like. All may be practiced while sitting comfortably or lying down in a peaceful, quiet place.

— Kuan Yin's Nectar of Immortality —

You do this version of the visualization lying down. Take a few slow, deep breaths and mentally travel throughout your body. Notice any areas where there is tension or pain. Relieve these areas by breathing into them and releasing tension or stress as you exhale. After you have mentally moved through your body, adjust your position to make sure that you are resting comfortably.

Now visualize Kuan Yin above you, floating on a magnificent lotus flower and moving toward you. See her immersed in radiant light and smiling at you. In her hand she carries her beautiful nectar vase made of fine jade. See yourself smiling back at her. Realize that Kuan Yin knows exactly where you experience pain or have any other problems, and watch as she begins to pour nectar onto these ailing places, drop by drop. The nectar has a calming effect and a refreshing quality that nourishes and rebalances the areas of your body that need it. Feel each drop of nectar relaxing you as you regain your inner peace. While you experience Kuan Yin's loving compassion, you may chant one of her mantras. When she has finished blessing you with her nectar, thank her and smile at her. Then watch as she floats away on her lotus flower.

As a sitting variation of the nectar meditation above, imagine Kuan Yin floating on her lotus throne directly over the crown of your head, pouring her nectar onto your seated body. Feel it replenishing you as you become a vessel filled with its radiant essence. Now feel the nectar flowing out of your body through your feet, flushing all negative energy and suffering into the earth, which absorbs and neutralizes the liquid harmlessly.

— Kuan Yin's Helping Hand —

Assume a comfortable meditation posture, close your eyes, and think of a problem that you want to solve. Create a symbol of it in your imagination. Now call upon Kuan Yin, and ask for her help in solving this problem. In your mind's eye, see the sky opening and Kuan Yin's fine and elegant hand appearing, extended toward you. Put the symbol into her hand and observe as she grasps it and pulls it back into the sky. Notice how relieved you feel that Kuan Yin has lifted your problem from you. Take some extra time to meditate, and open yourself to a thought or an instruction from Kuan Yin that may further support your problem solving.

You may be able to find a special porcelain figure of Kuan Yin, as I did in Los Angeles's Chinatown, that offers another way to invoke her helping hand: one of her hands can be removed from the sleeve. When you have a special request, ask Kuan Yin for help with it, then take out her hand as a token of your request and hide it until she has fulfilled your wish.

— Full Moon Kuan Yin —

Take a few deep breaths and relax. With your inner eye, imagine your thoughts and emotions taking the form of an ocean at night. You may be amazed at the turbulence of your internal sea, at how loudly it roars. Suddenly, notice that the energy is changing—you perceive stillness, deep serenity, and protection. Riding on a single, perfect lotus petal, surrounded by radiant light, Kuan Yin floats toward you across the now-gentle waves of the ocean.

She is so happy to see you! Her compassionate eyes are filled with tears of joy, like those of a loving mother reunited with her child. Feel how deeply you are touched by her compassion, and watch as a ray of rainbow-colored light pours from her heart into yours. As you receive Kuan Yin's light, you may wish to chant one of her mantras. When your entire body has been filled with the light of her compassion, thank her deeply. Now watch as she slowly begins to dissolve in this light, until only the soft night sky above the ocean remains. Feel embraced and protected by this dark yin (female) space, and connected to eternity. Feel the deep silence of pure *being*, and rest in it for a while. Then take a deep breath, and come out of meditation.

To strengthen your inner light, practice this meditation in the dark of night, or use a blindfold.

— The Peacock Feather: Kuan Yin's Eye —

The peacock feather is considered a powerful symbol of Kuan Yin. This stems from a legend in which a peacock becomes her attendant on earth (see page 131).

Take about fifteen to twenty minutes to do this meditation. Assume your favorite seated meditation posture with a small table or cupboard placed at arm's length in front of you. Stand a peacock feather in a small vase or incense holder to make sure that it is upright. The end of the feather should be at eye level so that you can easily focus on it. Relax your eyes, and gaze at the feather, drawing your attention to the "eye" in its center. Let the muscles around your eyes soften and relax. You may also quietly recite a Kuan Yin mantra during this session.

A more advanced practice is to look at the peacock feather without blinking. Keep your eyes relaxed, and let your tears flow. Do this for just a few minutes at first to prevent tension in the eyes. Afterward you may cool your eyes by applying cotton wool eye pads that have been dipped in water; you may also add a few drops of pure rose water.

The Cosmic Ear of Kuan Yin

In the Lotus Sutra, which describes many of her physical manifestations, Kuan Yin is referred to as the bodhisattva who "observes the cries of the world"—an indication of her special hearing abilities.

It is practically impossible for most people to imagine this kind of hearing. The human world is awash in a multitude of sounds and tones, and this fabric of sound is folded into the sounds of the universe. Surely, it takes a special cosmic ear to identify the cry for help of a needy being in this sea of auditory vibrations. Not only is Kuan Yin able to radiate loving compassion, but she also has an exceptional ability to listen for our need.

Here is a practice you can use to get in touch with the cosmic ear of Kuan Yin. Sit or lie down for meditation in a quiet place. Breathe, relax, and let yourself enter a deep state of contemplation. Take your time. When you feel very calm and peaceful, focus your consciousness on listening for the all-embracing sound that emanates from the human world—it is a fusion of all the sounds ever made by people.

After your session, take some notes; you will have many insights, especially in the beginning. As you repeat this practice, you will find your mind becoming even calmer. Some people say that they first perceive this sound of the human world as an accumulation of single sounds and tones, which gradually melt into the enveloping sound of the primordial syllable OM. As I described at the beginning of the book, this was my own experience as well, long before I met Kuan Yin.

This way of listening can be transcended even further. Kuan Yin reached her higher stages of enlightenment through the discipline of hearing, as described in the text of the Shurangama Sutra. Following are some of the core teachings of the sutra.

Shurangama Sutra and the Enlightenment of Bodhisattva Kuan Yin

The Buddha once asked twenty-five bodhisattvas to explain their practices for attaining enlightenment. These practices were captured in the Shurangama Sutra. He then asked Manjushri, the bodhisattva of wisdom, to assess them. Manjushri deemed Kuan Yin's method the most suitable for the human beings of this world.

Kuan Yin's Shurangama Sutra is profound and complex, and exploring it in its entirety is more than we can do here. But we can make a start. We can examine the first of several core statements in the sutra that are attributed to her—the basics of Kuan Yin's meditation as she herself taught it. We will look deeply at the specific words she uses as she begins to describe it, and with this new understanding you can begin to walk Kuan Yin's path in your own meditations. But first, let's recall the essence of the Buddha's teachings.

Essentially, the goal of Buddhism is liberation from suffering, which is caused by our attachments to the delusions that our minds create. The mind attempts to attach to all kinds of "objects," whether they are external to us (experienced through our sensory organs) or internal (knowledge or ideas).

When the mind attaches to an object, it believes that it is real, and from this the four mental poisons arise: ignorance, greed, hatred, and suffering. But in fact, many of our life experiences are based on assumptions and perceptions that don't correspond to reality. Buddhism offers us ways to reverse and

Jewel in the countryside: Figurine with embroidered brocade robe in a tiny temple in the Hong Kong area.

dissolve this attachment to delusion, through practices such as meditation and contemplation that enable us to achieve a state of single-mindedness. This involves much more than simply sitting quietly; instead, we must focus our mental energies step by step. But it is well worth the effort. Whenever we reach the goal of single-mindedness, our delusions and attachments disappear without a trace.

— Kuan Yin Describes Her Practice —

First, I focus on the hearing consciousness and allow the sounds that are contacting the ear to flow off, and thus sound objects subside and disappear. Then, since ear-contact and hearing objects produce no effect, the mind remains in a state of clarity, and the phenomena of motion and stillness no longer occur.

Meditative absorption gradually deepens; ultimately the distinction between hearing consciousness and the objects of hearing consciousness are no longer in existence. . . .

So this is where we learn that hers is the path of hearing. It consists of five stages; at each one of these, the mind's deluded attachment must be dissolved. The stages are: sound, hearing, hearing ability, hearing consciousness, and the "I." Our least subtle and weakest attachment is to the first stage, sound. Our subtlest and strongest attachment is to the final stage, "I." Extinguishing the "I" is the most difficult step.

We tend to confuse the first four types of hearing attachment, especially in the beginning. So let's go over them as we explore the hearing path.

— Sounds as "Hearing Objects" —

A very long time ago, Kuan Yin was human. She began her path to enlightenment by identifying the varying levels of hearing attachment.

Kuan Yin often meditated near the ocean. As she awoke one quiet morning, she heard a remote sound—the ocean surf breaking the silence. After a while, the sound ceased and silence returned. Then, as the sound of the surf arose again, the silence disappeared, and Kuan Yin realized that she was hearing two things: the ocean surf and the silence. But it was impossible to hear both simultaneously, because each time the sound of the ocean grew, silence ceased. And when silence again arose, the sound of the surf vanished.

— The Nature of Sounds and Hearing Ability —

Investigating further, Kuan Yin realized that both sound objects had something in common: they arose, and they ceased. It was her human sense of hearing that made it possible to listen to both of these sounds; she could detect the surf, and she could detect the silence. If her ability to hear had ceased when the surf ebbed, she would not have been able to perceive the subsequent silence, or the surf when it resumed. Thus it was that Kuan Yin realized that her sense of hearing was constant—not dependent on the presence or absence of sounds.

— A Way to Listen—

When sounds come and go, rise and fade, we should be aware that we have the ingrained habit, the familiar pattern, of following them. We attach to them and assume that they are real. As a result, we develop an illusionary attachment to them.

But let's think about this a little differently. If, for example, someone rang a bell and then asked, "Do you hear the bell?" you would say that yes, you did. If he asked you the same question after the sound vibrations had faded, you would say no, you could no longer hear it. Using your powers of language you could describe exactly what had happened—the bell sounded, loudly at first, and then gradually fell silent.

Now, how would you respond if you were asked a different question after the bell sounded: Do you hear *something?* As long as you could still perceive the sound, you would say "yes," and of course you did. After the sound had waned, you would answer "No, I don't hear anything." But this is not true! You may not hear the ringing bell, but you can still hear "something."

Even when there are no sounds for us to perceive, our sense of hearing allows us to discern silence. This sense persists regardless of the presence or absence of sound vibrations—it perceives the ebb and flow of passing vibrations, but hearing, itself, does not change. Even people who could once hear but have become deaf retain their sense of hearing, continuing to hear sounds internally, whether awake or dreaming.

So now we have identified the difference between sound and our ability to hear it. Sounds are impermanent; they come and go. But the gift of our sense of hearing is continuously present, with no starting point and no end.

— Hearing Ability and Hearing Consciousness —

When we perceive sounds externally, through our ears, it is our brains that enable us to experience them. Sound waves cause the eardrum to vibrate; this stimulates sensory cells, and the auditory nerve transmits this information to the brain. So we can say that hearing is the process of experiencing sound through the combined activity of our ears and our brains. Because stimulation ultimately occurs in the brain, this aspect of hearing might be called "hearing consciousness."

Our hearing consciousness is active even without any external sounds registering in our ears: when we hear an inner voice, the sound of silence, or voices in a dream.

— Kuan Yin's Practice of Dissolving Sound Attachments —

Let's summarize the four levels of attachment we have discussed so far: *Sounds* are the impermanent objects of hearing, which continuously arise and disappear. We may identify them through physical *hearing* (ear and brain activity) and our *hearing ability*, or through our *hearing consciousness* (which also perceives nonphysical sounds). Once we are able to differentiate between these aspects of hearing, it is easier to grasp the beginning of Kuan Yin's teaching. Let's look again at her first sentence: *First I focus on the hearing consciousness and allow the sounds that are contacting the ear to flow off, and thus sound objects subside and disappear.*

We have five sensory organs (eyes, ears, nose, tongue, and skin) in addition to the mind with its world of thoughts and ideas. In Buddhism these sensory organs are considered "gates" or "doors." Kuan Yin's focus is the door of the ear: the sounds that touch it create a point of contact between the sensory organ and its object (in this case sound).

Then, since ear-contact and hearing objects produce no effect, the mind remains in a state of clarity, and the phenomena of motion and stillness no longer occur.

When sounds fade, Kuan Yin neither grasps them nor dwells on them, as doing so would cause her mind to stir. Her goal is to let go of any outside sound her ear perceives so that she may achieve stillness and clarity of mind. This practice might appear simple, but it is actually rather difficult to achieve. We are accustomed to identifying sounds, connecting to them, describing them as words and sentences, and attributing meaning to them. And it is exactly this identification that causes mental irritation, emotional upheaval, and suffering.

— Listening to Language —

When someone utters a short sequence of syllables we have never heard before, we may be able to repeat them. Let's use the example of *Om Mani Padme Hum*. The syllables do more than simply pass through our ears; we memorize them, connect to them, and, in this case, come to regard them as a mantra. At this point, the mantra's deeper meaning doesn't even matter; what matters is the intensity of our attachment to the sounds. And let's remember that to dissolve our attachment, we must allow the sounds to simply cease.

In the initial stages of learning a foreign mantra, we may have little difficulty in letting go of the sounds because, though we can identify the syllables and imitate them, we do not attribute meaning to them. At times, then, we can allow these combinations of sounds to pass fairly easily through our consciousness.

But there are still many levels of attachment. When we begin to ascribe meaning to the mantra, we become more deeply attached. When we interpret the meaning in different ways, or judge the value of the mantra, this is another kind of attachment. If we invest in it emotionally, this is yet another way that we hold on.

— Letting Go of Sounds —

When you consider all of these ways that we attach to sounds, you may think that it's virtually impossible to let go of them, because our minds will continually attempt to connect syllables or snippets of sound to a certain context. But there are also moments when we do succeed in letting go. We may not pay attention to background sounds like traffic, children's voices, or someone coughing if we are trying to understand someone who is speaking to us. Our attachment is to the sound objects the speaker creates—and we must attach, or we will be unable to respond to what the speaker says. Under these circumstances, we can readily block out background sounds and not even retain memory of their existence. So it is possible to let go.

— Going Beyond the Attachment to Hearing Objects —

Next, Kuan Yin says: *Meditative absorption gradually deepens; ultimately the distinction between hearing consciousness and the objects of hearing consciousness are no longer in existence. . . .* When we continuously practice letting sounds cease and letting the objects of hearing disappear, we reach a state in which our hearing consciousness becomes free from hearing objects and the ear's contact with outside sounds. Our hearing consciousness calms, and our mind becomes clear. We no longer perceive the movement of sound vibration, nor do we perceive silence, as silence can only be noticed in contrast to sound. Then we can experience one of the states of *samadhi* (deep meditative absorption).

To reach this stage is a great accomplishment, and we have only addressed two of the five stages of deluded attachment described at the beginning of this passage—attachment to sound and attachment to hearing. Still, dissolving them offers considerable relief from our worldly suffering, and we can then proceed further on this path of deepening meditation.

As you can see, Kuan Yin's enlightenment practice is challenging. Laypeople can barely grasp the Shurangama Sutra passages that follow those I have introduced here; they require intense meditation and study under the guidance of an experienced teacher. But having now gained some basic insights, we can take the first steps on Kuan Yin's path of hearing by following her initial instruction: *First I focus on the hearing consciousness and allow the sounds that are contacting the ear to flow off, and thus sound objects subside and disappear.*

— You May Follow Kuan Yin's Path —

Open yourself to Kuan Yin's guidance. Choose a meditation spot—near the ocean is ideal, but anywhere is fine—and sit for fifteen minutes or half an hour with your new awareness of sound and hearing. Your experience of the world will be transformed.

Creating Your Kuan Yin Altar

An altar is an important power spot in your home, a place for you to contemplate and honor the divine. An altar devoted to Kuan Yin embodies boundless compassion and provides protection for you and your loved ones.

In private homes, there are generally two main types of altars. One can be thought of as a "guardian" altar. It faces the main door, and the figurines upon it protect the entryway to the home. They welcome your human visitors as well as your personal guardian angels, and the positive energy they radiate counteracts any subtle harmful energies that may enter, such as negative thought projections or unfriendly intentions. The other kind of altar is the "family" altar, which is usually placed in a more enclosed space; ideally, it's in a separate room where people can spend time in meditation or prayer.

The ancient Chinese art and science of Feng Shui is key to creating your Kuan Yin altar. Feng shui brings harmony and balance into your environment, which is especially important when creating a sacred space. The principles of feng shui are complex, and if you are new to this discipline some of my suggestions may surprise you. It may help to think about it this way: you will be controlling the way energy flows around your altar, ensuring that the energy of the items upon it, as well as that of your spiritual practice there, is preserved and concentrated.

Following are some guidelines for creating your altar. The layout of your available space may make it difficult to implement them all, and that's fine; simply incorporate as many as you can, and be assured that you will create a very powerful space.

• It is best to place your "guardian" altar just off to one side rather than directly in front of the main door. Strong Qi energy (life force energy) enters there; this is like a form of energetic attack. Be sure that there is a solid wall or a divider behind it to form a firm backing.

Kuan Yin holds the Golden Essence Pearl,
surrounded by incense smoke.

- If the layout of your space is such that you have no choice but to place your altar in a direct line from a door, put a small table or a plant between it and the door, a little distance in front of it. This will slow down the incoming flow of Qi.

- When positioning statues or figurines on the altar table, always put them a bit closer to the back wall than to the front of the altar.

- You might enjoy adding the element of light to your altar. Your light source can illuminate it around the clock, like the sanctuary lamp or eternal flame of the Christian tradition. A small, soft light is best.

- Do not place your altar in the bedroom. It's perfectly fine to have decorative figurines in the room, perhaps on a bookshelf or a table. But an altar, a space that contains beloved statues, candles, incense, and other items that are meaningful to you, is spiritually charged. It is said that it will attract wandering spirits, whose energies may affect the quality of your sleep.

- Keep your altar clean and well maintained; this reflects purity of mind.

- Your altar needs to be grounded. Never set it on a shelf above a door, for example, where people will pass under it. It should be placed on a solid table or in a special cupboard.

- There should be no heavy ceiling beams in the altar area, nor should the altar be placed in the space below a staircase. Both of these large structures will suppress its energy.

- Make sure that there are no sharp corners or other pointed structures aiming toward your altar; according to feng shui principles, they will "attack" it.

- Avoid placing your altar near drainage pipes or an enclosed chimney. The flow of energy from these structures has the effect of disturbing and draining the positive energy you are creating.

- Also avoid setting it up opposite a bathroom or any other space that emits stagnant or unclean energies; do not place it against a bathroom wall.

- The altar should not be placed immediately next to a window. The concentrated Qi energy it will contain escapes faster through windows.

- Altars made from wood or other natural materials are best, and most beautiful. Plastic altars should be avoided, as plastic has very low energy.

- Ideally, the altar should follow traditional auspicious measurements. You can find details in many textbooks on feng shui. The feng shui "ruler" is 16$\frac{15}{16}$ inches long; one approach you can take is to build your altar in multiples of this length. Eight other auspicious measurements for tables and cupboards are: 25½ inches, 27 inches, 32½ inches, 42 inches, 44 inches, 52 inches, 61 inches, 78 inches, and 85 inches. These can be any dimension of your altar: height, width, or depth.

- Your altar can be very simple, or you can adorn it with an abundance of beautiful ornaments—it is entirely up to you. Follow your intuition and your heart. Avoid including any large mirrored surfaces, though, as the energy of statues or figurines will be disrupted by their reflective qualities.

- Because an altar often contains incense and candles, it includes the element of fire. If your altar has these things, do not place it near an aquarium or a big fountain; there will be a clash between the elements of fire and water.

- According to the Feng Shui system of the Eight Life Situations, the northwest direction is attributed to helpful people and mentors. Hence, an area in the northwest part of your room or home is ideal; there, your altar will receive enhanced support from the celestial beings.

Auspicious Times for Spiritual Practice

Your altar is a place for meditation, contemplation, and other spiritual practices. An especially auspicious time for a long, intensive practice is during the full moon. In addition, there are three holidays each year during which Kuan Yin (or Avalokiteshvara) is traditionally honored with recitations of the Lotus Sutra or the Great Dharani of Compassion. These holidays are dedicated to her birthday, her enlightenment, and her eventual final entry into Nirvana. On these days many Asian temples offer devotees a large vegetarian banquet. For a list of auspicious dates, see **www.kuanyin.info**.

— Statues and Figurines —

Just as feng shui principles can be used to create the best possible altar space, there are principles that apply to the statues or figurines that you will place upon it as well. Here are a few tips.

Ideally, your statue should be made from wood or stone. Wood represents growth and creativity. Jade is a gemstone that is specifically attributed to Kuan Yin, and it has strong protective power. Quartz crystal and amethyst also make wonderful spiritual statues. White or light-colored marble represents purity and solidity, while white porcelain is a symbol of innocence. Ceramic and porcelain figures can be fragile, so make sure that they have a wide base or pedestal for extra stability.

Do not put a statue that is obviously damaged on your altar—one that has big cracks or chipped areas, for example. It will be neither beautiful nor powerful.

Place your statues at eye level or higher. Remember, they represent celestial beings who gaze compassionately down upon us.

— Blessing Your Altar Statues and Figurines —

A statue is even more powerful once it has been blessed and "activated" by a priest, a master, or another person of high spiritual rank. You may ask a temple priest to bless your Kuan Yin statue or figurine. He will do this by dipping a willow branch in holy water and sprinkling the water upon it. Some priests or spiritual masters will chant a prayer and softly blow this energy toward the statue in a blessing. After the blessing ceremony, wrap the statue carefully in a cloth, take it home, and put it on your altar. Think ahead about where you will place it: it is best if you do not move it once it's in position.

Another way to activate your statue is to briefly touch it at the crown, the third eye, both eyes, the heart, and the base. In this way, the eyes of the figurine are opened spiritually. Some sensitive people are able to perceive a glow from these activated eyes. You can also touch these same areas with a dot of vermillion paint, but this should only be done on materials that the rich, red color cannot penetrate—glazed porcelain, for example.

In my travels, I have found several kinds of Kuan Yin altars. You may wish to adopt one of these approaches when you create your own space for Kuan Yin.

— The Basic Elements of a Chinese Altar —

In Chinese or Taoist tradition, the altar usually has three levels, and statues are placed upon it in a certain hierarchy. At the top level, Kuan Yin, Amitabha, and other bodhisattvas find their place. The middle level is dedicated to the ancestors—it contains special plates upon which their names are engraved. The lower level is reserved for the Earth God. Fresh fruits, candles, small lotus-shaped lamps, and incense burners may also be placed on the altar. To avoid fire hazards, small electric lamps are frequently used in lieu of candles, and electric candles and incense burners are available as well.

— The Basic Elements of a Buddhist Altar —

With this kind of altar, the statue to be worshipped stands upon a table or a cupboard shelf. A *thangka* (a picture on a scroll) showing a buddha or bodhisattva hangs on the wall, either above it or beside it. Seven small cups filled with seven offerings are placed in front of the statue. Cups contain clear water, scented water, flowers, and incense. One cup serves as an oil lamp, and one contains food—for example, sweets. The last cup holds a white snail, a symbol of divine music.

— The Basic Elements of a Simple Kuan Yin Altar —

As we have seen, Kuan Yin loves water, and clear, pure water symbolizes a pure mind. You can place at least one beautifully crafted cup filled with fresh water on your simple altar, and change it daily. A Kuan Yin altar will always benefit from fresh flowers; roses or peonies will support her soft, female energy. Fine silk flowers such as lotus or peony are also a good choice. A delicate incense placed in a pretty burner will clear the space, and a beautiful altar cloth will honor your statue.

— The Kuan Yin Home Altar in Asia —

Miniature altars that hold one or several small, and often kitschy, Kuan Yin figurines, artificial flowers, and a tiny incense burner can be found everywhere in Asia: in homes, offices, and restaurants. Frequently, these altars are hidden on a high shelf. It is said that the mere presence of Kuan Yin brings luck; the statue does not need to be worshipped daily with incense or offerings in order for the people in her presence to receive her blessings.

Visiting a Buddhist or Taoist Kuan Yin Temple

Your fascination with Kuan Yin may one day take you to a traditional Buddhist or Taoist temple, so I'd like to give you an idea of what you might expect to find there and how to enter and be in this space respectfully.

The entrance door to Chinese temples is often painted with guardian or lion symbols for protection. Usually, it has a high wooden threshold that prevents negative energies from entering the sanctuary. Take off your shoes and leave them at the entrance to the temple.

Enter the temple respectfully and with the intention of praying to Kuan Yin or asking her to grant a wish. In many temples, a large incense burner is placed in front of the altar inside the shrine. You may pick up three incense sticks, light them, and put them between your palms in an upright position at chest

Famous triad: Kuan Yin is on the left, Avalokiteshvara in the center, and Bodhisattva Mahasthamaprapta is on the right, representing the power of wisdom and recitation. These statues face the entrance of an ancient temple in Colombo, Sri Lanka.

level. Then bow three times, in front of the altar and give your prayer or wish to Kuan Yin. Take a moment to experience your connection to her; then place the incense sticks back into the burner.

At many large temples, the burners are placed outside the entrance to the main shrine to prevent fire hazards. If this is the case, stand outside with your incense and bow, facing the statue inside. Make your wish and leave the incense behind in the burner before entering the shrine.

You may also find a Chinese oracle for divination at the temple that you may use. To begin, you will toss two pieces of wood that resemble the halves of a potato onto the ground while asking whether this is an auspicious time to do divination. If the pieces of wood drop with the same side up, permission to use the oracle is granted. You may then pick up a quiver that contains a hundred bamboo sticks, each marked with a number. Hold the quiver in a slightly tilted position in front of you and shake it rhythmically until one or more sticks begin to move up the inside of the quiver. After some time, a stick will drop from it; in rare instances, two or three sticks will fall to the ground together. The first stick to fall provides the answer to your question.

The number on the stick refers to a divination poem, which may be found in a cupboard with a hundred pigeon holes or picked up from a small counter. These days, divination poems are printed in both Chinese and English. There is a common temple oracle as well as a special Kuan Yin oracle. The poems have hidden meanings and usually give indirect clues about whether your question will be answered or your wish fulfilled. Large Asian temples also host professional fortune tellers who can provide you with further details and advice.

When your request has been fulfilled, or even before if you can, visit the temple again to show your respect and gratitude. Bring an offering to place on the table in front of the altar; fruits such as oranges, apples, or grapes are popular offerings, as are flowers.

Tales and Legends of Kuan Yin

 There are countless tales and legends about Kuan Yin. Each describes an aspect of her superhuman powers to help people—to save lives, make peace, or pave the way toward spiritual enlightenment. The most popular legend is of Princess Miao Shan, who is considered the greatest manifestation of Kuan Yin, and who contributed to her importance in China (see The Legend of Princess Miao Shan, page 18). But I have encountered many more tales from the wealth of Kuan Yin legends, several of which follow. These charming stories demonstrate how this goddess's extraordinary abilities have fascinated her followers for centuries.

Kuan Yin with the Fish Basket

There once was a village near the sea where people argued constantly. Kuan Yin appeared there in the form of a pretty girl selling fish. The people approached her curiously.

The girl told them, "My fish are not meant to be eaten. I want you to buy them and release them back into the ocean." Although no one wanted to buy fish from her merely to set them free again, the young girl came with her fish basket every day, and each time more admirers gathered around her.

One day the pretty girl with the fish basket announced that she would marry the man who could recite a particular chapter from the Lotus Sutra. She recited the text herself, and the very next day half of her eager suitors were also able to recite it. But she was not yet satisfied; she then wanted to hear longer passages

from the Sutra. In the end, only one suitor, a young man named Malang, pleased her when he recited the complete Lotus Sutra by heart. Malang was overjoyed that this intelligent and beautiful young woman was to become his wife. And indeed they were married, but she died the same day and was buried immediately.

Though brokenhearted, Malang continued to recite the sutra texts. In this way he helped his neighbors to understand the Buddhist teachings, and peace began to spread among them. After some time had passed, a monk appeared in the village and asked that Malang's wife's coffin be opened. When the people did as he asked, they found that the bones inside it were made of pure gold. The monk declared this a sign that the young woman had in fact been the bodhisattva Kuan Yin. The townspeople built a temple to worship her and thank her for the peace they had found. Some time later, Kuan Yin appeared once again to young Malang, and he became a buddha.

Above: Stone relief: Panel decoration at the Kek-Lok-Si Temple on the island of Penang, Malaysia.

Below: Statue made from wax: Devotees in Thailand offer small pieces of gold leaf, placing them on the head or face of the figurine.

Kuan Yin Who Does Not Want to Leave

Once during the Liang dynasty (about AD 502–549) a Japanese monk named Hui Erh studied Buddhism in China, acquiring many scriptures. He was an enthusiastic devotee of Kuan Yin and wished to take a beautiful statue of the bodhisattva back to his homeland. He lived in central China at Wutai Mountain where there was a small temple that had a statue of Kuan Yin. He admired it so much that shortly before his departure, he decided to steal it.

On the way to Japan his boat passed the island called Mei Cen. As he approached a mountain on the island, called Potala Mountain, his boat suddenly stopped, as if it were somehow stuck. Then a mighty storm came up, and the monk became frightened. Countless lotus flowers made of iron began to unfold upon the surface of the water. The monk immediately understood these messages: he must leave the statue behind on Mei Cen, for the karma of his people had not yet ripened, and they were not ready for the statue or the teachings of Kuan Yin. Despite his love for the statue, Hui Erh made up his mind to give it to the inhabitants of Mei Cen. No sooner had he done so than the iron lotus flowers disappeared, as quickly as they had emerged. (This part of the ocean would later be called "Lotus Sea.")

The stormy waters calmed, and Hui Erh came ashore on Mei Cen at the famous "Cave of Tidal Sounds." There he met an old fisherman who kindly provided his cottage as the first Kuan Yin shrine on the island. Today, the Bukenqu shrine of Kuan Yin Who Does Not Want to Leave can still be found on this spot. Many people have visited it, receiving visions of Kuan Yin and seeing their entreaties of her fulfilled. Hui Erh never did return to Japan as he had intended, instead becoming the abbot of this temple. More and more temples were built on the beautiful island and many Kuan Yin legends spread across it. At times the island held more than a hundred temples.

By now you may have guessed that Mei Cen is now called Putuo Shan, and remains to this day the "home" of Kuan Yin.

Kuan Yin and Her Guardian Wei Tuo

One day Wei Tuo, an engineer who built houses and bridges, traveled to the banks of a wild river. It was extremely dangerous to cross the water there, impossible even by boat. Wei Tuo was walking along the riverbank reflecting upon what type of bridge he could build there, lost in thought, when suddenly he saw a beautiful girl. She was standing in a boat in the middle of the river! Wei Tuo did not know that this attractive woman who stood so serenely amid the raging waters was Kuan Yin, and he immediately fell in love with her.

Kuan Yin pretended that she was looking for a groom and told Wei Tuo and the other men on the shore to throw coins at her. The one whose coin hit her would become her husband. But none of the coins touched her—they simply dropped into the boat. Kuan Yin announced that the money that had begun to cover the bottom of the boat should be used to build a bridge across the river to save lives.

The engineer wanted to have this girl at all costs and asked the Taoist Lu Tung Bing to help him. With the aid of Lu Tung Bing's special powers, Wei Tuo was at last able to hit Kuan Yin with one of his coins.

When Wei Tuo asked her to marry him, she finally disclosed her identity. Still he would not part from her, deciding instead to stay and be her protector, and she accepted him as one of her regular attendants.

We can still see representations of Kuan Yin and Wei Tuo today in many temples. They stand with their heads turned toward one another, like husband and wife. In some temples Wei Tuo is the guardian of the Buddhist teachings and head of the celestial generals, and stands in a hall facing the main shrine. He is placed back to back with the fat, happy version of the Buddha, who represents prosperity and abundance and is the first one to greet temple visitors.

Kuan Yin and the Lotus Flower

Shortly before her enlightenment, Kuan Yin was sitting in meditation upon a rock near a lake when she overheard two people in conversation. As she listened with pleasure to their melodic voices, she heard one of them say, "Look at these marvelous lotus flowers unfolding above the surface of the water!"

"Yes," the other one said, "and on each of them sits a buddha." After looking at the flowers for a while, the first person said, "But look—one of the flowers is empty."

That night Kuan Yin dreamed that her heart transformed into a white lotus, radiantly unfolding its petals. In its center she recognized the silhouette of a buddha. She approached the lotus to look at the buddha more closely, and saw that she herself was to occupy the last empty flower in the lotus pond from then on.

Kuan Yin and the Peacock

At a time when there was much discord on earth, Kuan Yin descended from the sky and taught people how to live together as friends. As long as she was present, they displayed a compassionate and loving attitude toward each other. But when she returned to the heavens and left people to find their own way, they resumed their arguing and fighting. She came back to earth several times in order to settle arguments and teach people how to deal with one another more peacefully. Still, each time she left earth, they fell back into their previous state, creating ever more conflicts for themselves.

Kuan Yin reflected on this dilemma, and soon found a solution: she announced that she would appoint a guardian to watch over the peaceful earth in her absence. She summoned a large, dull brown bird with long tail feathers to her side. She rubbed her smooth jade hands over her face and then along the bird's feathers. Instantly, they shone in beautiful colors, and at the end of each tail feather was a clear, radiant eye. From then on, the peacock would observe all the people on earth and inform Kuan Yin about any misbehavior.

In this way the peacock became Kuan Yin's attendant and her guardian on earth. He was delighted by his new task, joyfully displaying his tail, and Kuan Yin was able to return to the heavens and fulfill her other duties there. So wherever we see peacocks, we should remember that Kuan Yin is compassionately watching over us.

The peacock is also said to be the earthly manifestation of the phoenix. His feathers are talismans that protect us from accidents, poisoning, diseases, and all other disasters. The feathers also represent compassion and immortality, and can absorb negative energies, protecting those who wear them.

The Monk with the Water Vessel

A young man suffered paralyzed legs, and longed to be healed. He decided that he would recite the Kuan Yin Sutra (the Lotus Sutra) continually for three years in the hope of a cure. One day a monk appeared before him, holding a water vessel. The young man asked the monk where he had come from, and he answered, "You have been calling for me again and again; that is why I am here now."

The young man bowed and asked the monk, "Please tell me. What kind of negative karma have I accumulated in a past life that now my legs must be paralyzed?"

The monk replied, "In a past life you caught and tied up many beings; this is the consequence of those actions. But close your eyes now, and I will heal you."

When the young man closed his eyes, he felt as though long nails were being pulled from his knees. When it was over, he was able to walk again, and the monk had disappeared. Only then did he realize that he had met Kuan Yin and been blessed by her. In gratitude, he took the vow of a monk himself.

Kuan Yin with the Mirror

Kuan Yin once appeared in a busy town as a pretty woman who owned a beautifully crafted mirror. She sat down beside her mirror and told everyone that she was willing to sell it for a thousand yuan. When people heard the price, they declined her offer indignantly, saying that it was much too high. "But," she told them, "this is no ordinary mirror. It has the power to show its owner the past and the future."

Many people wanted to test her claim, and one man said that he would pay three yuan to look into it. She agreed. A line formed, and by nightfall thousands had looked into the mirror. Still, no one wanted to buy it; they did not grasp that they had been given the gift of being able to see into many dimensions.

Finally the woman stood to leave and put the mirror into a box. Suddenly, she had three faces! The people then realized that the mysterious woman had been Kuan Yin, and indeed had the power to provide them with insights into their pasts and futures. And so they erected a temple with a triple-faced Kuan Yin statue inside.

Enemies from a Past Life

During a time when China was suffering from rebel attacks, there was a man named Chen who was a serious devotee of Kuan Yin. He had built an altar, and every day he made smoke and candle offerings to her. One night Kuan Yin appeared to him in a dream and said, "One of the rebels will come to your house and try to kill you." Chen awoke in shock, and prayed to her all day long for protection.

The next night Chen dreamed of Kuan Yin again, and this time she told him, "You killed this rebel in another life; so he is unconsciously trying to kill you in order to compensate for your karma. But I will do my best to help you. The man is called Wang Zhan. He comes from the province of He Nan and was an orphan; he only joined the rebels because he was impoverished. He will come tomorrow, and you should have a big dinner ready for him. Remember that friendship can change the heart of even the worst enemy." Then she disappeared.

The next day, Chen sent his family to a safe place and stayed behind to prepare a banquet. Soon he heard the rebels shouting, and one of them kicked the door open. Chen asked him, "Are you Wang Zhan from He Nan who was an orphan? I have been waiting for you; let us eat together." Wang was very surprised, but confirmed his identity and accepted Chen's invitation. While they were eating, Chen told him about Kuan Yin's appearance in his dreams.

At the end of the banquet Chen rose from his chair and knelt down in front of Wang Zhan. "I owe you a life, as I killed you in a previous life. Please kill me now to erase this karmic guilt forever."

Instead, Wang Zhan asked him to get up. He said, "My parents died when I was young, and in sheer desperation I joined the rebels. You are the first person ever to treat me in a friendly way. I am tired of killing and looting. Why should I kill you? You are my friend now."

Chen was deeply touched and replied, "I have some money here, why don't you take it and open up a small store? Then you won't have to be a rebel anymore." Wang gratefully accepted his offer, and the men became friends for life.

Dragon Boy and Dragon Girl

A buddha went on a journey to seek disciples for Kuan Yin. Along the way he met a boy who had been brought to a temple to become a monk after his parents died. The boy seemed a suitable disciple, so the buddha told him about the compassionate bodhisattva Kuan Yin and suggested that they join forces to meet her.

Kuan Yin and her attendants: The dragon boy on the right has respectfully placed his hands together to greet her while the dragon girl on the left carries the dragon pearl inside a lotus flower. Idyllic temple garden at the Hsi Lai Temple, Los Angeles.

Together they climbed a mountain. On their way up, the buddha pretended to hurt himself, stumbling and falling into a canyon. Determined to save him, the boy jumped after him . . . and found himself held in the arms of Kuan Yin. Looking down into the canyon, he saw his own dead body lying there. So strong were his devotion and his desire to save the monk's life that he was transformed into the spiritual dragon boy Shen Tsai, and became a follower of Kuan Yin.

The female attendant of Kuan Yin is the girl Lung Nu, daughter of one of the four dragon emperors. When one of her dragon brothers transformed himself into a fish to cross the ocean, he was caught by a fisherman and offered for sale in the marketplace. But Kuan Yin appeared and freed the boy. The dragon emperor was so happy to have his son back that he promised to protect Kuan Yin and to receive the Buddhist teachings from her. In recognition for her help he sent her a luminescent pearl. His daughter Lung Nu insisted on bringing it to Kuan Yin personally, instantly grew devoted to her, and became her disciple.

Putuo Shan: Kuan Yin's "Residence"

 If there is one place on earth where Kuan Yin takes center stage, it is on the Chinese island of Putuo Shan, the place that is widely considered to be her residence in this world. It has a mystical history, and today it is home to numerous devotional sites where Kuan Yin is honored and people seek her blessings.

The Four Buddhist Mountains

First let's look at Putuo Shan from a wider Buddhist perspective. According to Chinese tradition, mountains are thought of as sacred places where heaven and earth meet, and they are often the sites of popular retreats for both Taoist hermits and Buddhist monks. In Chinese, the word *shan* ("mountain") denotes a single peak as well as a group or a chain of mountains. "Sacred mountains" usually have special shapes or are located in special places. Today there are four sacred Buddhist mountains, which have been consecrated to the four great bodhisattvas.

Wutai Shan, the Buddhist mountain of the North in Shanxi province, is where Bodhisattva Manjushri is said to have manifested when the Buddha shone a ray of light from his third eye. With his sword of understanding, Manjushri cuts through ignorance.

Jiuhua Shan, Buddhist mountain of the South, is located in Anhui province. It is dedicated to Bodisattva Kshitigarbha, who is also called "Earth Buddha" or "Guardian of the Underworld."

Emei Shan, Buddhist mountain of the West, lies in the Szechuan province. Bodhisattva Samantabhadra, the "protector of the teachings and the teachers," came from India to settle here, riding on a white elephant with six teeth.

Putuo Shan, Buddhist "island mountain" of the East, is in Zhejiang province. This island is dedicated to Kuan Yin, who is said to have reached enlightenment there.

The History of Putuo Shan

This beautiful island, with its dramatic canyons, mysterious caves, and golden beaches, has been considered a sacred place for over two thousand years. Over time, it has carried several different names that reflect its natural beauty—among them, White Flower Mountain. During the first century AD the famous alchemist An Chi Sheng lived here, making medicines and pills that promised immortality; he himself is said to have lived for several hundred years. Up until the Tang dynasty, the highest mountain on the island was named for another famous Taoist alchemist, Mei Fu, who came to Putuo Shan for a retreat during the first century BC with the same goal in mind—to create remedies that held the power to bestow eternal life.

By the end of the Tang dynasty in the late eighth century, both the legend of Hui Erh, the monk who brought the first Kuan Yin statue to the island, and the sutra texts about Kuan Yin (at that time still in her original male form as Avalokiteshvara) had spread, and the island had become widely known as a pilgrimage site. The Flower Ornament Sutra (Avatamsaka Sutra), which was translated into Chinese by the end of the eighth century, describes how the pilgrim Sudhana, on the advice of Manjushri, the bodhisattva of wisdom, journeyed to a mysterious island then called Potalaka. His intention was to meet Bodhisattva Avalokiteshvara there. The sutra describes Potalaka as a place made of jewels and adorned by an abundance of trees, flowers, gardens, ponds, and streams. Avalokiteshvara explained to Sudhana that beings on the path of compassion were reborn on this island, which he called "Buddha Land." Sudhana visited a total of fifty-three spiritual masters there, all of whom instructed him on his path to enlightenment. During the following three centuries the Avatamsaka Sutra became very popular, the connection between Potalaka and Putuo Shan grew, and many people made the pilgrimage to the island.

A lesser-known text, the Sutra of the Thousand-Armed and Thousand-Eyed Kuan Yin, describes Buddha Sakyamuni, the former Prince Siddhartha, who was said to have imparted his teachings at the palace of Kuan Yin on the island

Island landscape of the South China Sea.

Left: Altar at the Immortals' Well: From here you can travel through time back to the beginnings of Taoism. Center: A glimpse of the marble Kuan Yin: On this New Year's Day thousands of pilgrims enter the nunnery. Right: Monks reciting sutra texts: In the background glows a golden statue of One-Thousand Armed Kuan Yin.

of Potalaka. This led to speculation that Potalaka might have been off the south coast of India, or perhaps at the former palace of the Dalai Lama in Tibet. Still, its association with Putuo Shan remained.

In the fourteenth century a legend evolved in which Kuan Yin guided people to her three most important pilgrimage sites. When the city of Hangchow was destroyed during the Yuan dynasty (1271–1386), a Kuan Yin statue mysteriously disappeared from the Shang Tien Shu monastery, which had also been destroyed. A reward was offered, the statue was found, and it was brought to the new Hsi Tien monastery. When it was consecrated there during an official ceremony, three rays of light suddenly emanated from it—one ray illuminated the Hsi Tien monastery itself, the second pointed to the old monastery of Shan Tien Chu, and the third beamed in the direction of Putuo Shan.

Putuo Shan continued to dominate as the authentic home of Kuan Yin, and more and more monasteries and hermitages were erected there. Then, during the fifteenth century, pirate raids destroyed all but one of the three hundred temples that had been built on the island. Most of them were later rebuilt with the help of an emperor who provided financial support.

During the Ming (1386–1644) and Qing (1644–1911) dynasties, Putuo Shan became an important trading port. Ships from Japan and Korea stopped there for customs inspections when importing their goods into China. Traders frequently used this opportunity to visit the shrine near the Cave of the Tidal Sounds, asking for blessings for their travels on the sea.

Up until the nineteenth century, Buddhist texts and travel diaries emphasized the merits of making a pilgrimage to Putuo Shan. By that time, the island was better known and more popular than Hsian Shan Mountain on the Chinese mainland, which, according to legend, is where Princess Miao Shan retreated to attain enlightenment after her flight from a burning monastery. We find Kuan Yin shrines on other great spiritual mountains of China, but none are as renowned as Putuo Shan.

In 1925 the ninth Dalai Lama visited Putuo Shan. His words, engraved in Tibetan on a stele erected beside a large memorial gate near the ocean, can still be seen today: "The islets in the ocean are so exotic and beautiful, and this trip is blessed by Bodhisattva Kuan Yin."

When the communists took power in China in 1949, there were still more than two hundred temples on Kuan Yin's island and more than two thousand monks and nuns living there. Most temples survived the Cultural Revolution (1966–1975), but afterward they were destroyed, and their occupants were relocated by the communist regime. Since then, some of them have been allowed to come back, and some novices have been admitted again.

Putuo Shan remains a vibrant center for pilgrims seeking Kuan Yin's blessings and those interested in learning more about her legends and manifestations. At the same time, in recent years it has felt the strain of a flood of tourists drawn by its beautiful beaches. Moreover, thanks to its picturesque landscape, Putuo Shan is often selected as a site for filming movies. As a result of all of this activity, the island's spirit-nourishing silence and rough natural beauty are hard to experience during the warmer seasons. Still, those who come to Putuo Shan with the focused intention of tuning in to the energy of Kuan Yin will definitely have an opportunity to enjoy it in the more remote areas, and on less populated beaches.

Putuo Shan's Sacred Sites

Despite modernization and tourism, the island has preserved much of its magic. The spirit of Kuan Yin still brings life to the island and manifests especially in those places where natural energies prevail. I have traveled to Putuo Shan twice and have been awed by the representations of Kuan Yin I have found there and by her powerful presence, which can be felt everywhere.

At present there are three main temples and eighty devotional sites on the island. The temples on the northern peak—Puji, Fayu, and Huiji—are among the most impressive and magnificent in all of China. There is a saying there: "Each corner of the mountain holds a temple, and if you get lost, a monk (Kuan Yin) will appear."

At Dragon Bay to the south, also called Heaven's Gate, the largest Kuan Yin statue stands facing out to sea—a prominent landmark one can see on the boat ride into the harbor. Farther up the island at the huge cliff of the Buddhist Cave, water breaks in an eternal variety of sounds, innumerable voices whisper and sing, and you can feel Kuan Yin's divine energy. Buddha Peak, the highest point on the island, has some wild spots; gnarled trees obstruct the path, and everything seems to breathe with the energies of nature spirits.

At the Pilgrim Staircase, the stairs to the shrine above meander amid a jungle of old trees and giant rocks that all seem to be alive. There are several springs on Putuo Shan that are said to contain Kuan Yin's sacred waters. At sunset on the picturesque Thousand Steps Beach, it is not uncommon to find a few monks dressed in black returning to their monastery, soundlessly swaying across the golden sand.

Fayu temple is a favorite spot. There is a magnificent statue of the Buddha there, and nine golden dragons dance around the golden essence pearl on the ceiling. There are other landmarks nearby as well, including South Sea Kuan Yin, a fifty-five-foot-high gold-plated bronze statue enthroned on a six-foot-tall lotus; she leans forward slightly, as if standing against the sea winds. Also nearby is the Bukenqu shrine, home of Kuan Yin Who Does Not Want to Leave, where the Japanese monk Hui Erh placed the first Kuan Yin statue to arrive on the island.

The Pavilion of Kuan Yin's Voice, nestled between rocks beside the sea, is a welcoming place to listen for Kuan Yin. The Immortal Well is another highlight, one easily overlooked unless you are on foot. Located in a cave hidden in a small wood only a few hundred steps away from the sea, it is the place that the Taoist An Qisheng, the Confucian scholar Mei Fu, and the Taoist sage and shaman Ge Hong are all said to have dwelled, preparing their medicines and immortality pills.

Pantuo Rock, also named Diamond Rock, is a huge rounded boulder that balances on a natural rock pedestal, touching only at a few hands' breadths. Kuan Yin is said to have taught other bodhisattvas while sitting atop this rock. A legend tells of animals coming here to listen to Kuan Yin's sutra teachings: fish, whales, and sea turtles all came swimming to hear her.

Above: The statue in the Fayu main shrine is one of the most beautiful representations of the Buddha I have ever seen.

Below: Large Japanese statues made of gray granite.

And off the southern coast you can see the small island of Luijia Shan where, according to legend, Kuan Yin stayed for a while before taking one giant leap onto Putuo Shan. A rock on the shore of Luijia Shan is said to bear her footprint.

It would be fair to say the Putuo Shan is simply enchanted with the presence of Kuan Yin, the compassionate goddess of antiquity who is cherished by people around the world today. I hope that you, too, can one day make the journey to Putuo Shan to receive blessings from the great bodhisattva Kuan Yin, whose brilliant light illuminates the hearts of people everywhere. But no matter how many trips we take to visit Kuan Yin in the external world, the most exciting and profound journey is the one that leads inside. There, at the deepest core, our potential for inspiration, enlightenment, and liberation lies dormant. Ultimately, we don't have to travel anywhere—we carry Kuan Yin's compassionate heart with us always.

Namo Kuan Shi Yin Pusa!

Conclusion: Living Kuan Yin Day by Day

I once traveled to the Abbey of Einsiedeln in Switzerland to see the famous Black Madonna statue there. As I stood before it, transported by the sublime voices of the abbey's choir, I came to understand that I was in touch with one of the archetypal "gateways" to feminine power. The dark-skinned Madonna was stunning. She was dressed in intricately embroidered brocade robes and surrounded by golden carvings in swirling shapes that reminded me of Asian depictions of water and clouds. Surrounding her were ornaments shaped like hearts with bright flames leaping from them. This was more than a statue of the Madonna: it reached beyond its form, connecting to the consciousness of the divine feminine.

While contemplating this wondrous shrine, I had a flash of insight about yin and yang—the principles of female and male—and I knew that the female principle is the basis of everything. Dark in a positive but mysterious way, and deeply nourishing, it is the sustaining stillness from which the primordial ray of light bursts into being: female giving birth to male, darkness giving birth to light. This is the ancient Mother: patient, embracing, caring, and compassionate, blessing by her mere presence.

In the sacred space of the Madonna's altar, I was reminded that mother images of every tradition and culture share this same mystical source, and that this source is available to each of us. It must be, for it is a part of us. We all have the capacity to offer one another the nourishment of the divine feminine.

As the Black Madonna at the abbey was a gateway to the female principle for me in that moment, Kuan Yin is such a gateway in my life—always. In this book, I have endeavored to give you many pathways to her. As you contemplate the Kuan Yin images you have found here, as you chant the mantras, practice the visualizations, or create a sacred space for Kuan Yin in your home, it is my hope, dear reader, that you will come to know Kuan Yin—and that by tapping into the consciousness of healing and compassion day by day, you yourself will become the gateway to these qualities for others.

— Appendix A: Kuan Yin Variations in Brief —

Here for your quick reference you will find brief descriptions of forty-one manifestations of Kuan Yin. The illustrated contemplations chapter introduced you to thirty-three of these forms in greater depth; I have added an additional eight common forms to the list. When you find a statue or figurine that intrigues you, you may use these descriptions as clues to which manifestation of Kuan Yin it represents.

Traditionally, there is no set order to Kuan Yin's forms; I have numbered them purely for the sake of reference. For each, I briefly describe her body posture and any symbolic objects she may carry. You will find the meanings of these symbols in the next section beginning on page 154. Finally, I indicate the origins of some of these forms, either from the Lotus Sutra or Chinese and Indian legend.

The complexity of Kuan Yin is evident in the variety of her iconography; her forms are myriad. In the Lotus Sutra she first appears as the male Avalokiteshvara, who then begins to assume several female forms. In some passages the bodhisattva manifests as a human male or female—a general, a layman, a nun, or a girl—while in others he is described by his qualities as a savior, not by his appearance. In later Chinese and Japanese collections of Kuan Yin images, these roles and qualities are connected with a special iconography. For example, the message of Kuan Yin with the Lotus (number 5, page 40) is immediately conveyed by the symbol she carries: the lotus, representing purity, enlightenment, and the bodhisattva vow.

1. Dragonhead Kuan Yin

Kuan Yin stands or sits on a dragon, riding on clouds or on water. Her hands form various mudras and/or she holds a willow branch or her nectar vase.
Lotus Sutra: She appears as a *naga* (serpent deity) or *yaksha* (nature spirit).
Chinese legend: Saves distressed ships.

2. Kuan Yin of Non-Duality
She sits on a rock, holding a *vajra* (diamond scepter); alternatively, she stands on a lotus leaf with her arms lowered and her hands folded in front of her. Lotus Sutra: Appears as a deity with a vajra; protects from demons.

3. Kuan Yin of Unity
She stands on a thundercloud, displaying the mudra of unity. Alternatively, she sits upon a lotus on a storm cloud in the royal ease pose, both hands on her left knee, her left leg raised. Lotus Sutra: Protects from natural disasters.

4. Kuan Yin of Prayer
Sitting or standing on a lotus, she places her palms together in respect, greeting, or prayer. Lotus Sutra: Appears as a Brahmin, her hands corresponding to the Indian greeting gesture, *namasté*.

5. Kuan Yin with the Lotus
Kuan Yin stands on a floating lotus leaf holding a lotus flower. Lotus Sutra: Appears as a boy or girl.

6. Kuan Yin of Pure Water
She stands on a rock or on clouds, holding a bowl of water in her left hand and a willow branch in her right. Lotus Sutra: Protects from the dangers of water and natural disasters.

7. Mother Kuan Yin (also Kuan Yin of Liberation or Tara Kuan Yin)
She stands on a cloud or sits in meditation pose on a lotus in the sky. Lotus Sutra: Protects against bandits.

8. Kuan Yin of the Seashell
Kuan Yin sits in royal ease pose before an open seashell. Alternatively, she sits in meditation pose behind a giant seashell. Lotus Sutra: Appears as a buddha. Chinese legend: Protector of fishermen.

9. Kuan Yin of Fearlessness

She rides on a lion, her third eye open. She may have many arms holding varying symbols. Lotus Sutra: She appears as the celestial general Vaishravana, teaching the dharma. In this context she sits on a rock with both hands on her knee.

10. Kuan Yin of the Sutras

She stands or sits on a rock, holding a scroll in her right hand. Lotus Sutra: Appears as a *sravaka*, a disciple of the Buddha who attained enlightenment by listening to his teachings. Chinese legend: Holds a stick topped with a skull.

11. Kuan Yin of the Rock Cave

Kuan Yin sits at the entrance to a cave in the royal ease pose or in lotus posture. Lotus Sutra: Protects from poisonous animals such as snakes and scorpions.

12. Kuan Yin of Universal Compassion

She stands on a rock or a peak, with arms crossed and concealed in her sleeves. Alternatively, she holds a nectar vase with both hands. Lotus Sutra: Appears as Mahesvara, the highest deity in the world of form.

13. Kuan Yin of the Six Time Periods

She stands with a sutra scroll in her hand, often surrounded by the symbols of the sun and moon. Lotus Sutra: Appears as a layperson.

14. Kuan Yin of Serenity (Calming Kuan Yin)

She sits on a rock with palms together. Alternatively, her hands are placed upon a slate rock. She rests in deep contemplation. Lotus Sutra: Savior of victims of disaster.

15. Kuan Yin of Joy (Kuan Yin of Happiness)

On rainbow-colored clouds, she sits in the royal pose. Alternatively, she sits in contemplation at a lotus pond with her legs crossed and one hand supporting her head. Lotus Sutra: Savior of needy or worried beings.

16. Kuan Yin of Treasures

Kuan Yin sits in contemplation upon a rock in the royal pose. One leg is bent, and her elbow rests on her knee. Lotus Sutra: Protector of treasure hunters; appears as an elder.

17. Longevity Kuan Yin (Thousand-Armed Kuan Yin)

Either seated or standing, she has many arms, thus symbolizing the Thousand-Armed Kuan Yin. Alternatively, she stands behind a rock with her head resting on one hand, the other arm supported by the rock. Lotus Sutra: Protects from poisons and curses.

18. Kuan Yin with the Blue Neck

She sits upon a rock in the royal pose, one hand on the knee of her bent leg. Her neck has a blue spot or is entirely blue. Her head may also be blue. She resembles the Indian god Shiva. Lotus Sutra: Appears as a buddha.

19. One-Leaf Kuan Yin

Standing or sitting in the royal pose on a lotus leaf, she holds various symbols, such as a pearl, a nectar vase, or the Joo-I scepter (see Appendix B). Lotus Sutra: Savior of the shipwrecked.

20. Water-Moon Kuan Yin

She stands upon a lotus flower, holding a lotus or willow branch and the nectar vase. Lotus Sutra: Appears as a buddha on a lotus leaf with hands clasped, looking up at the moon.

21. Kuan Yin with the Fish Basket

She is the daughter of a devout Buddhist who sells fish on the beach (see Kuan Yin with the Fish Basket legend on page 127). Lotus Sutra: Stands on a huge carp, holding an empty basket, which symbolically serves as a trap for spirits and demons. Saves humans from *rakshasas* (giants), *nagas* (serpent deities), and demons.

22. Waterfall Kuan Yin

She sits on a rock contemplating a nearby waterfall. Lotus Sutra: Transforms threatening fire into water.

23. Medicine Kuan Yin
Usually standing, she holds a medicine pill, the wish-fulfilling pearl, or the nectar vase. Lotus Sutra and Chinese legend: Cures people of diseases.

24. White-Robed Kuan Yin
Wearing a white robe and a veil, she sits or stands upon a rock. Some images show her holding a lotus flower. This is considered to be one of the original forms of Kuan Yin. Lotus Sutra: Kuan Yin appears as an ordained monk or nun.

25. Kuan Yin with the Willow Branch
She holds a willow branch and the nectar vase. The willow branch stands in the vase as a symbol of enlightenment. Alternatively, Kuan Yin holds only a willow branch. Lotus Sutra: Appears as Brahma, the creator deity.

26. Four-Armed Kuan Yin
Sitting or standing, she holds various symbols to ward off negative forces. Chinese legend: Causes the sword of the executioner to break into pieces.

27. Anu Kuan Yin
She sits with her left leg bent and both hands resting on her knee. Alternatively, she sits cross-legged on a rock surrounded by water, hands upon her knees. Lotus Sutra: Protects from the dangers of water. Indian legend: Sits at the shore of the sacred Lake Anu in the Himalayas.

28. Kuan Yin with a Halo of Fire (Kuan Yin of Complete Light)
Surrounded by a halo, she sits upon a rock with palms together. She can have many arms. Lotus Sutra: Shatters the weapons of attackers.

29. Kuan Yin of Virtue
Kuan Yin sits upon a rock holding a scepter in her left hand and a lotus in her right. Alternatively, she holds only a lotus flower. Lotus Sutra: Appears as a celestial general.

30. Leaf-Robed Kuan Yin

She sits or stands cross-legged on a rock, with her hands concealed in her sleeves. In this form, she protects from diseases. Lotus Sutra: Appears as Indra, the Indian god of natural forces, or as Sakra, the king of Tavatimsa heaven at Mount Sumeru, the spiritual summit of the world.

31. Kuan Yin on a Lotus Leaf

She either sits in the royal pose or lies on her side with one hand supporting her head. Alternatively, she sits cross-legged on a lotus leaf with her palms together. Lotus Sutra: Appears as a prince teaching the dharma.
Chinese legend: Damaged Kuan Yin statue is found and repaired by a devotee.

32. Dragonfish Kuan Yin

She stands on a giant fish with the head of a dragon, holding the pearl and nectar vase or, according to legend, a golden hook. Alternatively, she rides a giant carp. Lotus Sutra: When standing on the carp, she protects from dangerous water animals.

33. Kuan Yin with Children

Kuan Yin stands holding a child; sometimes she is surrounded by several children. This is one of the most popular Chinese images. Lotus Sutra: Gives sons; protects pregnant women and mothers.

34. Kuan Yin with Color-Glazed (Incense) Bowl

She may stand on a floating lotus leaf. She holds a color-glazed incense bowl with both hands. In this form she helps prolong life. Lotus Sutra: Appears as the divine Isvaradeva or a king.

35. Joy of Wandering Kuan Yin

In royal pose, she sits on a rock or on rainbow-colored clouds. One hand is placed on her raised knee, and the other on the rock or cloud to support her body. Lotus Sutra: Protects from falling off a mountain.

36. Kuan Yin as the Wife of Malang
She stands with her palms together at the center of her body, wearing a celestial floating robe. In this form she does not wear the ornaments of a bodhisattva (jewelry around her neck, wrists, or ankles). Lotus Sutra: Appears as the wife of an official. Chinese legend: The wife of Malang, the suitor who managed to quote the sutras by heart.

37. Kuan Yin Riding the Unicorn
Kuan Yin sits on a unicorn, holding the wish-fulfilling pearl and the nectar vase. She tames demonic and chaotic forces with her compassion. (This Chinese form, as well as the next four, are not mentioned in the Lotus Sutra.)

38. Kuan Yin on the Lion
She rides a lion. In one hand she holds the wish-fulfilling pearl or another symbol. The other hand holds the mudra of granting a wish.

39. Kuan Yin with Rocks, Bamboo, and the Ocean
Kuan Yin sits in contemplation near the ocean with her legs crossed in the lotus pose, surrounded by a natural coastal landscape and bamboo. Her arms are hidden in her wide sleeves. This is a popular Chinese image in which she has a dream or vision of an emperor.

40. South Sea Kuan Yin
She holds the dharma wheel in her left hand and her right forms the mudra of fearlessness. In this manifestation she preaches the Buddhist teachings. This is the form that was selected for the huge landmark statue on Putuo Shan.

41. Kuan Yin as Princess Miao Shan
She is shown standing, with the long flowing robes of a Chinese princess and her hair piled high. Like the wife of Malang, she does not wear the bodhisattva ornaments and thus cannot easily be identified as Kuan Yin.

— Appendix B: Kuan Yin's Symbolic Objects —

Here is a list of symbols that are associated with Kuan Yin. They can be found in images, tales, and sutra texts.

Arrow: Summons friends.

Ax: Protects from suppression by authorities and institutions.

Bark (small ship) of enlightenment: On this boat, Kuan Yin escorts the souls of devotees to reach the Pure Land (the Western paradise ruled by Buddha Amitabha).

Basket: A symbolic trap for spirits.

Bell: Represents wonderful music.

Bird (pigeonlike): The light within the darkness—Princess Miao Shan or Kuan Yin—dispels human delusion with its songs. (See also Sun disk with bird.)

Book, precious: Attaining of great knowledge.

Bow: Glorious career.

Bowl, jeweled: Container for healing waters or remedies against diseases; symbol of overcoming disasters.

Buddha with a halo on a lotus: Numerous lives under the guidance of the buddhas.

Children: Creative power and continuation of the clan.

Club: Control over spirits.

Conch, white: Can be blown like a horn for calling upon *devas* (divinities) and other positive beings.

Crown: The crown or diadem of Kuan Yin usually shows a picture of Buddha Amitabha, her spiritual father who rules the Pure Land.

Dew of compassion (amrita): Bears universal healing powers. Eliminates suffering, purifies body, speech, and mind, and has a life-prolonging effect. (See also Nectar.)

Dharma wheel: Symbol of the Buddhist teachings.

Double-edged scepter *(vajra)*: Weapon against demons.

Dragon (Chinese: *lung*): A lucky celestial animal that represents spirituality, wisdom, power, and divine transformation.

Dragonfish: Sea monster that may be dangerous to humans.

Dragonhead symbol: Taming of wild animals.

Duster: Made from white horsetail hair, for chasing away difficult situations.

Fish: A Chinese lucky symbol representing prosperity and abundance. In Buddhism the ever-open eyes of a fish represent eternally active compassion. A huge carp (koi) that is able to subdue demons and malicious beings is one of Kuan Yin's riding animals.

Grapes: For bountiful harvests.

Hare: See Moon disk with hare.

Hellebore: Fights dishonesty.

Hook: Protection provided by *devas* (divine beings) and dragon kings.

Jade bangle (triangle-shaped with rounded corners): The support of sons and daughters.

Jewel, wish-fulfilling: Fulfills helpful wishes on the path toward enlightenment.

Joo-I scepter: Protects from dangers; symbol of prosperity and the Buddhist teachings.

Lion: A guardian of buildings, he stands for the majestic power of the Buddhist teachings; his roar represents the truth.

Lotus: Symbol of purity, enlightenment, and the bodhisattva vow. The white lotus represents the accumulation of spiritual merit, the blue stands for rebirth in the Pure Land, and the purple for the awareness of the presence of bodhisattvas.

Lotus pedestal: Kuan Yin's foot on the pedestal symbolizes power over the three mental poisons: greed, hatred, and ignorance.

Mirror, round with handle: Symbol of wisdom.

Monk's staff with iron tip: Represents compassion and the desire to protect others.

Moon disk with hare: Neutralizes poison, cools fever.

Nectar: A liquid, also called "amrita" or "dew," with healing and nourishing qualities, infused with the compassion of Kuan Yin. It is the liquid contained in her nectar vase.

Nectar vase: Symbol of longevity, virtue, and compassion. The vase shape is similar to Chinese ritual drinking vials (The Chinese word is *kuang* (See also Willow branch).

Ornaments: Jewelry around Kuan Yin's neck, wrists, and/or ankles indicates that she is a bodhisattva.

Palacelike pavilion: Indicates that one has spent many lives in the palace of the buddhas.

Peach: Symbol of longevity and the season of spring.

Peacock: This bird corresponds to the mystical phoenix or garuda bird. According to legend, the peacock evolved from a feather of the mystical bird. Peacock feathers are worn as talismans to protect from accidents, diseases, or other mishaps. They symbolize compassion and immortality, as they have the ability to absorb negative energies.

Pearl: In Buddhism, also called the "wish-fulfilling" jewel. When held by Medicine Kuan Yin, it represents a medical pill. In Taoist terms, the pearl represents immortality.

Peony: Represents love, luck, and female beauty.

Phoenix: Celestial lucky bird, the female counterpart of the dragon. May have multiple heads. The red phoenix represents the fire of the South.

Prayer beads (*mala*): Support by the buddhas of the ten directions. The devotee who uses prayer beads is received in the Pure Land of Buddha Amitabha.

Rice bowl or rice sheaf: Represents fertility and food as well as livelihood.

Rock: Close connection with nature.

Rope: Binds harmful influences.

Seal, precious: Carved from stone and used as a signature, the seal represents the gift of eloquence.

Sun disk with bird: Victory over darkness and blindness.

Sword: Subdues water spirits.

Tiger: King of the terrestrial animals. The white tiger represents the West and thus the spiritual world. According to legend, a white tiger carried Miao Shan away when she faced execution.

Turtle: Sacred animal, symbol of longevity, energy, and stamina.

Unicorn: Mystical dragon horse, usually with scaly skin and antlers. The male has an additional horn on the forehead. It is said to embody all positive characteristics and the gentleness of the animal kingdom.

Vajra dagger: Weapon to subdue enemies.

Vase: Symbol of longevity, virtue, and compassion.

Water: Purification, blessings, and healing. Brings emotional and spiritual peace to all beings.

Water bottle: Rebirth in Brahma-loka (a type of misty Buddhist heaven).

Wheel: The spreading of knowledge and Buddhist teachings leading to liberation.

Willow branch: Stands for healing, compassion for the sick, flexibility, wish fulfillment, exorcism of spirits.

— Appendix C: Kuan Yin's Mudras —

Here is a visual summary of the mudras you will commonly find in representations of Kuan Yin.

Fearlessness: The right hand is raised, and the open palm faces forward

Granting a wish/showing compassion: The right palm faces forward; fingers are pointing down.

Meditation: Hands are placed in the lap, one upon the other, with palms facing up.

Prayer and respect: The palms are placed together, fingers pointing up. (Also compare to the Indian greeting gesture, *namasté*.)

Protection from evil forces: Arms are lifted to the height of the chest; palms are parallel and facing each other.

Teaching: The right hand is raised, the palm faces forward, and thumb and forefinger are touching.

— Bibliography —

Beer, Robert. *The Encyclopedia of Tibetan Symbols and Motifs*. Boston: Shambhala, 1999.

Blavatsky, Helena Petrovna. *The Secret Doctrine*. Pasadena, CA: Theosophical University Press, 1999.

Blofeld, John. *Bodhisattva of Compassion: The Mystical Tradition of Kuan Yin* Boston: Shambhala, 1988.

Boucher, Sandy. *Discovering Kwan Yin: Buddhist Goddess of Compassion*. Boston: Beacon Press, 2000.

Chamberlain, Jonathan. *Chinese Gods*. Kelana Jaya, Malaysia: Pelanduk Publications, 1987.

Chün-fang Yü. *Kuan Yin: The Chinese Transformation of Avalokiteshvara*. New York: Columbia University Press, 2001.

Karcher, Stephen. *The Kuan Yin Oracle: The Voice of the Goddess of Compassion* London: Time Warner Trade Publishing, 2003.

Laotse. *Tao Te King. A New English Version*. New York: HarperCollins, 2000.

Leighton, Taigen Daniel. *Faces of Compassion: Classic Bodhisattva Archetypes and Their Modern Expression*. Ilford, UK: Wisdom Books, 2003.

The Lotus Sutra. Translated by Burton Watson. New York: Columbia University Press, 1993.

Mascetti, Manuela Dunn. *Kuan Yin Box*. San Francisco: Chronicle Books, 2004.

Matsunaga, Alicia. *The Buddhist Philosophy of Assimilation*. Tokyo: Sophia University and Rutland, VT: C.E. Tuttle Company, 1969.

Mesco, Sabrina. *Healing Mudras: Yoga for Your Hands*. New York: Wellspring/ Ballantine, 2000.

Palmer, Martin. *Kuan Yin*. London: Thorsons Publishers, 1998.

The Shurangama Sutra. Burlingame, CA: Buddhist Text Translation Society, 2003.

Williams, C. A. S. *Outlines of Chinese Symbolism & Art Motives*. New York: Dover Publications, 1976.

— About the Author and Artist —

Daniela Schenker
. . . is a certified translator and has studied Asian traditions for more than twenty years. In order to deepen her knowledge of the interaction of cosmic energies, she has gone on numerous pilgrimages and journeys around the world and has studied Chinese and Vedic astrology. She works internationally as an astrologer, a Feng Shui consultant, and a holistic lifestyle advisor.

Antonia Baginski
. . . was born in 1968 in Munich. For more than ten years she has worked as a freelance artist in the fields of computer graphics, web design, and illustration. She finds further inspiration for her illustration work by regularly attending workshops at the Stepan Zavrel school for children's book illustration in Sàrmede, Italy.

Visit www.KuanYin.info
for information about products, trips, and events.

About Sounds True

S ounds True was founded in 1985 with a clear vision:
to disseminate spiritual wisdom. Located in Boulder,
Colorado, Sounds True publishes teaching programs that
are designed to educate, uplift, and inspire. We work
with many of the leading spiritual teachers, thinkers,
healers, and visionary artists of our time.

To receive a free catalog of tools and teachings for
personal and spiritual transformation, please visit
www.soundstrue.com, call toll-free 800-333-9185,
or write to us at the address below.

SOUNDS TRUE

PO Box 8010
Boulder CO 80306